HOW TO TAME THE STUDENT LOAN DRAGON

By

CHRISTINE A. KINGSTON, ESQ.

Copyright © 2021 by Christine A. Kingston, Esq. and Surf City Lawyers, APC All rights reserved. No part of this document may be reproduced or transmitted in any form or by any means, electronic, mechanical, photocopying, recording, or otherwise, without prior written permission from the author.

Legal Disclaimer

This book is not legal advice and no attorney-client relationship has been created. This book is for educational and informational purposes only. You should always seek the advice of an attorney before taking any action on the information provided.

Dedication

For my son Charlie who will never have student loans because I forbid them. This book is also dedicated to the nearly 43 million Americans with student loan debt.

Table of contents

Table of contents iv
Introduction 1
CHAPTER ONE 18
Hatching the Student Loan Dragon 18
    A. A Historical Look Back at Higher Education in the New World 19
    B. Low School Standards For Federal Student Loans .. 25
    C. Student Loans the Servicing Nightmare; The Rise of the Student Loan Dragon 28
    D. Out of Control Tuition 31
    E. Families Willing to Put Everything On the Line For One Child's Education 37
    F. How Can We Be Better Educated, and in the Process, Control the Consequences? 40

CHAPTER TWO 47
The Loan Dragon goes to College will explain Financial Aid and the FAFSA process with resources to successfully navigate that lair. 47
    A. An Education in Student Loans and the Business of Education 48
    B. Financial Aid and FAFSA® 50

C. Types of Education Loans.. 51

D. Resources to Navigate the Dragon's Lair 55

E. Sorting the Thunder of Dragons 59

F. Who Are the Players in the Student Loan Business? 61

G. A quick recap. 68

CHAPTER THREE 72

Taming The Federal Student Loan Dragon takes a detailed "How To" look at exploring consolidation, loan default, and alternative repayment plans. 72

A. A Primer on Defaulted Federal Student Loan Dragons 74

B. Good Standing Never Felt So Good......................... 77

C. Alternative Payment Plans—Options for Killing the Dragon Slowly. 85

D. Other Alternatives to Bankruptcy for Federal Student Loans.. 90

G. A Peek Into the Future 97

CHAPTER FOUR.. 99

Taming the Private Student Loan Dragons includes information on how to successfully navigate through collection laws, statute of limitations, Strategic default and negotiations to settle. 99

A. Private Student Loans 101

B. Collections for Private Student Loans.................... 104

C. Beware of Co-Signors and Think Twice Now 120

v

CHAPTER FIVE 122

The Parent Dragon Trap explains Parent Plus Loans and co-signed private student loans which burn families who try to make college work at any and all costs. 122

    A. Parent Plus Loans 123

    B. Refinancing Federal Parent Plus Loans to Private Loans 131

    C. Private Co-Signed Student Loans 133

CHAPTER SIX 135

Taming through Bankruptcy answers the million-dollar question: To bankrupt or Not to Bankrupt. This chapter will take a realistic look at this option once others have been exhausted. 135

    A. Student Loan Debt Can Be Discharged in Bankruptcy 143

    B. The Future of Student Loans in Bankruptcy 163

CHAPTER SEVEN 173

Dragon Birth Control (hahahaha) This Chapter is especially important for anyone who has not yet signed on the dotted line, with valuable "what to look for" tips. 173

    A. Before You enroll College 176

    B. Tips for Keeping College Costs Down 180

    C. Don't Piss Off the Teachers 181

    D. Avoid Scams and Bribes 183

  E. Questions to ask any professional before hiring them 189

CHAPTER EIGHT 190

The Tail/Tale So What? Why it matters. In Conclusion What do tame dragons eat? 190

  A. Why it Matters? 191

  B. Truth over Stigma 193

  C. The Bigger Picture 194

  D. Morality and The Price of Education 196

  E. The Future of Education Must Transform 201

NOTES 209

Bibliography 215

Acknowledgments 217

Resources 219

About the Author 220

Introduction
What the heck happened?

Perspective is everything. The student loan dragon started out as just another great government idea that everyone in the United States be given the opportunity to attend college. What happened since then is nothing short of a nightmare.

In 2004, total student loan debt was a whopping $346 billion. Today, it's an unbelievable $1.6 trillion. That's a 362% increase in fifteen years. At this rate, projections by World.edu say that by 2030 student loan debt will reach a record $17 Trillion! What started out as maybe a pet bearded dragon, has turned into an untamed, angry, aggressive and downright dangerous monster. This monster will be disastrous for the future health and financial well-being of our next generation. Panicked? Take a deep breath. The bad news is that there is a problem, and the good news is, there is a solution. There is a way to tame the dragon before we are all burnt to a crisp. In this book, we're going to provide you with all the information you need to tame the 'out of control' student loan dragon.

One of the reasons I became an attorney is to protect people from being taken advantage of. I know the feeling and vowed that I would dedicate my life to a field where I can make a difference. I know the government has certain duties and obligations, and at the same time, I feel that the student loan dragon has grown out of control, attacking the very people it exists to serve. There is a sense of injustice that must be addressed, and so with this book, we begin.

Are you feeling the heat from the student loan dragon? Are you feeling overwhelmed and anxious? Are you putting off getting married? Are you working full-time, but your entire paycheck is going to dragon food? Maybe you're a parent who felt obligated to pay for your kid's college education, without saving any money. Without savings, you proceeded to take out a Parent Plus loan, or co-signed on a private loan, so your children could have a better life, at any cost. Are you feeling the heat? Are you feeling trapped? Misled? The following true scenarios are to give you hope, because you are not alone. And wherever you are, that's the best place to start.

Carla's story:

All I wanted to be when I grew up was a doctor. I came to the United States as a Cambodian refugee and I am now a citizen. I knew that my future would be bright if I chose to get into the best possible schools.

I went to college and graduated in 1996. I signed up for a Chiropractic college because I was told I would be a doctor and be able to write prescriptions and practice medicine.

I realize now that the language barrier and subsequent misunderstanding cost me money and time because I found out that I didn't know that chiropractors were not medical doctors I left this school and never finished the program.

Yet, I was still determined to become a doctor in America, one of the most prestigious professions. I found Spartan Health Sciences University School of Medicine and started that program in 2002. I found out too late that this school's licensing program had been placed on the "Disapproved" list of the California Medical Board: "Neither education completed, nor diplomas issued by these schools will be accepted toward meeting the requirements for training and/or licensure in this state." Again, what I didn't know hurt me.

So, I never became a doctor, I'm a college professor now, with not only an unfulfilled dream, but to add insult to *injury, I have; more than $300,000.00 in student loans that I feel like I'll never be able to repay.*

Carla's American Dream was eroded by the actions of two opportunistic "for-profit" colleges. Some colleges and universities lack accountability to actually deliver a quality education. Furthermore, the government's low standards for issuing Title IV government student loans are adding to the problem, allowing students, especially foreign students, to become dragon bait What's missing is government oversight over the quality and accurate claims of professional schools and colleges. Moreover, there is no regulation of sky-rocketing tuition costs. In contrast, the insurance industry's premiums are highly regulated by government bodies. Perhaps it's time to apply similar attention to our country's education system.

Donnie and Sharon's story:

My husband and I never went to college and have nothing more than high school diplomas. I was working as a campus security guard and my husband was a tradesman. Like every parent, we want the best for our children and we were willing to sacrifice for their future. We felt obligated to pay for our son's college education, even though we didn't have the savings to pay for it. We took out "Parent Plus" loans for our son and borrowed $40,000.00, which turned into $57,000.00. After taking on this debt, my husband became permanently disabled and was later diagnosed with liver cancer. We had no money to take care of ourselves, let alone pay back student loans.

What's worse is our son didn't really want to go to college and hasn't used his education to further his career, only making a bad situation worse. We even tried to look into *alternative payment plans and were told that our loan didn't qualify.*

Donnie and Sharon are not alone. Today at least 3.4 million people hold Parent PLUS loans, owing nearly $90 billion, according to a November 2018 Report by the Brookings Institution, a public policy research group. So the good and bad news is, you're not alone. Generations are being trapped by the Federal Parent Plus Loans and private loan cosigner requirements.

Scott's story:

I love helping heal people so I became a Chiropractor back in the 90's. To obtain my degree, I took out a federal government Health Education Assistance Loan (HEAL) loan for, $86,989.00 and a private student loan for $259,500.00. I started my own practice and believed I would make enough money to pay back my loans. Life was good.

For the past 24 years, the chiropractic industry has taken many twists and turns, especially with respect to insurance reimbursement. Because I accept patients' insurance, it has become more and more difficult to make enough money to continue my practice. Every year it becomes harder for me to collect money from insurers or even charge a reasonable rate for each adjustment.

Back in the 90's I would charge $100.00 and today, I only collect $30.00 per adjustment with insurance. On top of that, changes in healthcare make it increasingly difficult to obtain insurance coverage for chiropractic services and more patients were forced to pay cash, which still doesn't cover my overhead. Unfortunately, they don't teach us how to make money in chiropractic school.

After two decades of hard work, my business was failing and so did my marriage. My life fell apart and my student loans fell into default. What they never told me was that if your HEAL loans go into default, they take away your ability to bill through Medi-Cal or other insurance programs, so I lost many of my patients when this happened.

So, after investing $347,000.00 in my career, and making payments on those loans for almost 25 years, and treating thousands of patients successfully, I still owe an unbelievable $450,000.00 and cannot afford to practice.

We enter college with a burning desire for a successful and prosperous life. We enter into the college and university process with high hopes and a belief that we will be able to repay our school loans, tame the dragons and win the tournament. Our vision may have been a bit blurred by our rose-colored goggles so that we didn't even look closely at the documents before signing. Furthermore, most professional schools don't teach us how to run a private practice or start a small business.

Nancy's story:

All I needed was two years of college for a certificate to be a radiology technician and take x-rays. I borrowed $20,000 in student loans and was told that I didn't have to make any payments while I was in school. Now I've graduated and my student loans are due, but the bill is saying I owe close to $40,000! How could my loan have doubled in two years?! What's worse is that this amount is equal to an entire year's salary. How will I live? How is this even possible?

Borrowing money for a college education is seen as a necessary requirement, for many, toward a worthy goal. Failing to understand the terms and types of student loans available can be a $20,000 decision, like Nancy made.

College is expensive enough without compounding interest being added to your loan, while you figure out how to graduate.

So, this is what the heck happened.

There is a common theme to each of these stories, which are representative of my clients' experiences, and from others whom I have encountered in and out of the courtroom. With every story, there is an underlying feeling of uncertainty, frustration and confusion that stems from believing that one has done everything right, but then something goes terribly wrong.

The famous proverb "ipsa scientia potestas est" was first quoted by Sir Francis Bacon and means, "knowledge itself is power." This tenet is what our education system is founded on.

A college education increases knowledge, and therefore, power, an important goal in life

The translation that lives in the American Dream is that every American can grab the brass ring of a better life through a college education. And for a while, the great American Dream flourished. "You get what you pay for, so get the best education from the highest-ranking school you can get accepted to," is what people bought into...literally! But now, we live in the age of bribes, scandals and $1.7 trillion dollars in student loan debt that grows $1,000.00 per second thanks to compounding interest. The cost of the average college degree is more than a year's salary upon graduation, forcing even baby boomers to delay retirement to repay their student loans.

You're now being punished for making the most important decision of your life and an investment in yourself. Your parents are being punished for feeling obligated to pay for your education at any cost. You didn't negotiate the contract, you just signed what was needed to get through the system. You may not have read all of the fine print, but should that result in being burned to a crisp? The good news is we realize we've summoned a dragon and we have a problem. Actually, we have several problems. Lots of problems.

> *Schools that mislead*
>
> *Low standards for quality of education*
>
> *Out of control tuition costs*
>
> *Student didn't read the whole contract*
>
> *Student didn't understand the contract*
>
> *Student didn't see the fine print*
>
> *Student had no knowledgeable about payback terms on loans*
>
> *New loan products that put parents' money at risk, not just students*
>
> *Families willing to make college work at any cost*

> *Graduates not taught and have no understanding how to start and/or run a successful business*
>
> *Changes in legislation and industry for the self-employed create income loss.*
>
> *New businesses that promise to help with student loans for a "fee" without making a difference.*
>
> *Ability to discharge student loans in bankruptcy has been slowly taken away since late 70's when Sallie Mae came into existence.*

Influencers and media continually telling the public that student loans cannot be discharged in bankruptcy is not 100% accurate. At present, it's difficult, but not impossible.

This book promises to deliver the tools you'll need for solutions that work and where to find them. And more good news, there are solutions to these problems!

Chapter 1—will give you a Brief historical look at student loans in the United States and how we can be better educated in the process of controlling the consequences.

Chapter 2— Financial Aid and FAFSA for college explained with resources to navigate that lair.

Chapter 3—takes a detailed "How To" look at taming the federal student loan dragon, exploring consolidation, loan default, and alternative repayment plans. Options for getting my loans under control?

Chapter 4—The Good news and the Bad news about Private Student Loans including collection laws, statute of limitations, Strategic default and negations to settle.

Chapter 5—describes The Parent Trap with Parent Plus Loans and co-signed private student loans which burn families who try to make college work at any and all costs.

Chapter 6—To bankrupt or Not to Bankrupt...that is the million-dollar question...This chapter will take a realistic look at this option once others have been exhausted. The future of student loans in bankruptcy. Now What? Is Bankruptcy the Solution? What I know from 10 years and more than $2 Million in student loans discharged in bankruptcy. How to discharge student loans in bankruptcy.

Why bankruptcy is the best place to process student loan debt relief plans. Would you believe that student loans once were included in bankruptcy? Undue Hardship, Totality of the Circumstances, and Unqualified Education Loans explained from a bankruptcy perspective.

Chapter 7— Dragon Birth Control (hahahaha) This Chapter is especially important for anyone who has not yet signed on the dotted line, with valuable "what to look for" tips. Before you sign on the dotted line (or Things I wish I should have known before I signed on the dotted line) is the chapter for those students and parents who are looking at loan options, with valuable "what to look for" tips.

Chapter 8—So What? Why it matters In Conclusion What do tame dragons eat?

By the time you finish, you will be armed with the facts and truth about the current student loan crisis reality, so that you can make well-informed decisions to tame your student loan dragon.

Let's get started.

CHAPTER ONE

Hatching the Student Loan Dragon

As we begin our discussion, we will deliver a brief historical look at student loans in the United States and how we can be better educated and, in the process, control the consequences. We review the historical rise of Institutions of Higher Education (IHE) creating low risk and guaranteed, therefore, easy money. The meteoric rise in tuition, fees, costs, interest rates generating extreme wealth for some at a multi-generational cost to others.

A. A Historical Look Back at Higher Education in the New World

In researching for this book, I discovered the Wikipedia History of Higher Education in the United States. Interestingly, higher education started as a religious means, during the Colonial Era, to train ministers. You see, higher education was actually set up for the elite, by the elite, in service to their offspring, to keep and maintain great power within their families. Religious institutions and wealthy families supported local schools, until Land Grant universities came on the scene in the late 1800's, which provided federal funding for schools specializing in agriculture and engineering. The purpose of these land-grant institutions was, "without excluding other scientific and classical studies and including military tactic, to teach such branches of learning as are related to agriculture and the mechanic arts…in order to promote the liberal and practical education of the industrial classes in the several pursuits and professions in life." —Title 7, U.S. Code. The problems with higher education institutions were that many of them did not have endowments like Harvard did, to help them when the Great Depression hit. Higher education began as a means of specialized learning based upon religion, power and wealth, then military. Today, in the midst of a pandemic, the global online education market will be worth $319+ Billion by 2025.

The Great Depression led to the New Deal when most schools had to scale back without an elite endowment like Harvard. Public colleges depended on legislative grants and ignored fund-raising and philanthropy. Colleges and universities across the country were cutting salaries and budgets and yelling pleas for emergency assistance that were rejected. The New Deal was No Deal for much too elitist higher education.

As author Daniel Clark asks in Creating the College Man, "Might not our present debates about the purpose and place of college education (what value it adds) be advanced by a deeper understanding of the genesis of the American embrace of college education?"

Americans have embraced college education due to the fact that it changes people's lives dramatically. So much so that families are willing to do whatever it takes to get them through. From college scandals, federal Parent Plus loans, to co-signed private student loans; some families are sacrificing, while others are throwing money into a system for the same result. Prestige and a better life for the next generation.

The famous proverb "ipsa scientia potestas est" meaning "knowledge itself is power" was first quoted by Sir Francis Bacon. Meaning: The phrase "knowledge itself is power" means that knowledge is the most powerful tool to achieve or do anything. The American ideal developed from these concepts. Our ideal was to achieve superiority by developing a nation of educated citizens. The seed of yet another great government idea that everyone should be able to attain a college degree if they wanted to. The great ideas are always followed by capitalistic greed and self-preservation over the greater good for the All. The world of those of means is vastly different than their fellow Americans. A more novel approach may be to consider one's vocation or station in the world in terms of natural talents and gifts and what the future evolution of mankind would require of us. Sure, it's a bit utopian, but a girl can dream.

The first government-backed student loans were issued in 1958 as an Act to strengthen the national defense and to encourage and assist in the expansion and improvement of educational programs to meet critical national needs; and for other purposes. Not long after came the Higher Education Act of 1965 and the student loan dragon was hatched. Initially, banks issued the student loans and the federal government would only step in as a guarantor, in the event of default. Higher education loans became the way to level the playing field between the elite, wealthy and the rest of us. In the early 1980's, the phenomenon that price equals prestige arose too and is still alive.

Congress of 1965 certainly did not have our current system status in mind when they created the federal student loan system. "Their intention was to assist Americans in bettering themselves, and thus the nation, through higher education; it was not to make them captive to an unethical financing system that penalizes the people who need aid most." Capitalism seems to take our great government ideals and throw it into a wood chipper that spits out unkept promises while chaining us all to an indefinite future of working for wages from a billionaire.

Today, so many of the 43 million borrowers feel remorse in their decisions in listening to those telling them to go to the best school their SAT scores will get them in to. Some are lured the most, by creature comforts. Students and their families had their American Dream in mind when they started their college journey of making a better life for themselves, their families and communities. They sacrifice their time, peace and sleep with the determination to succeed at any price. Sadly, that sage advice no longer works because the system is rigged in the favor of the house.

What we need is a new plan. A new vision for our future to save our children from oppressive debt, anxiety, stress and depression from the emerging division and infighting we currently see. Student loan debt is but the tip of the iceberg of issues needing our attention presently, but I can only tackle one dragon at a time.

B. *Low School Standards For Federal Student Loans*

The education system is rigged in the sense that you borrow money to attend college and the school gets paid immediately upon the disbursement of your loans. What obligation does a college or university even have to provide you with a quality education when they've already been paid and you have yet to receive your education? This is the first troubling issue.

In order to participate in the Federal Student Aid ("FSA") programs a school must demonstrate that it is financially responsible. To provide the Department of

Education with the information necessary to evaluate a school's financial responsibility, schools are required to submit financial information to the Department every year, which has nothing to do with the quality of the knowledge provided or degree obtained.

Eligibility for institutions to participate in Title IV Student Aid Program requirements are intended to provide a balance between consumer protection, quality assurance, and oversight and compliance in postsecondary education providers participating in Title IV student aid programs. This means that your college or university must meet minimum standards in order for you to obtain a federal student loan. An eligible Institution of Higher Education (IHE) may be deemed administratively incapable if it has a high Cohort Default Rate (CDR). Colleges are disciplined by the number of students who default on their student loans within a certain period of time. To keep default rates low many borrowers are continually placed into forbearance to keep loans in good standing while interest continues to accrue. This is just one strategy educational institutions use to manipulate the numbers for their schools. This works against borrowers who have been led into multiple forbearances without any servicing agent providing information on other payment alternatives that may be available. The current $1.6 Trillion in student loan debt is primarily from existing student loans whose balances are growing because the debt is not being re-paid or payments are so low that very little is applied to reducing principle.

As I finalize this work, we are in the midst of a global pandemic, a hotly contested election, and the exposure of systemic racism in this country. In 2020, student loan debt resolutions are being tossed around like a hot potato. For now, my advice is to stay the course on your current plan and we will wait and see what the next few years bring in terms of tackling this dragon. I am well aware of the pace this issue is moving at.

C. Student Loans the Servicing Nightmare; The Rise of the Student Loan Dragon

In 1972, Congress created the Student Loan Marketing Association, more commonly known as "Sallie Mae." This Government-Sponsored Enterprise (GSE) was designed to support secondary markets for student loans, as other GSEs were created to support home mortgage lending. Initially, Sallie Mae's business was relatively simple: it purchased student loans from—and made secured loans to—banks and other lenders. Over time, Sallie Mae began to issue Student Loan Asset-Backed Securities or SLABS and expanded into other parts of the student loan industry such as loan consolidation, servicing, and even college savings plans.

The government took steps to privatize Sallie Mae over time; by 2004, the privatization was complete, and the company had been renamed SLM Corporation. In April 2007, SLM Corporation reached an agreement in principle to be acquired by a group led by J.C. Flowers & Company, but the Flowers group later rejected the agreement, citing the credit crisis and passage of the College Cost Reduction and Access Act of 2007 under the agreement's material adverse effect clause. Following a lawsuit filed by SLM Corporation, the parties settled in January 2008.

Today, Sallie Mae is one of the largest lenders and servicer (through Navient) of student loans in the United States, though many other lenders are also vital participants. Sallie Mae is both the largest originator and holder of the

Federal Family Education Loan Program (FFELP) loans in the U.S., but concentrates on private loans these days.

Other familiar industry participants are Citibank, and Wells Fargo, but there are many newer lenders in the student loan marketplace today, which can be found online, like SOFI Lending who seems to be advertising by suggesting they have a way for you to get to your financial goals by taking a loan with them. Seriously? You buy that?

Servicing problems have had serious consequences to borrower's credit and balance owed. For example, if a borrower fails to renew their income-driven repayment plan eligibility, the payment will likely skyrocket and unpaid interest gets capitalized and tacked on to current loan balances. Servicers have abused forbearances on student loans because they accrue interest and the balances increase. When the schools are the lender on Perkins Loans, they favor a forbearance to manipulate their default rates. The entire servicing system is inconsistent and confusing due to the sheer volume of servicing companies under contract with the federal government. Some borrowers even struggle to understand what they really owe when their getting multiple bills from multiple servicers each month. Overwhelmed borrowers may inadvertently miss payments. Loan Servicers also provide different and conflicting information to borrowers about their loans and options.

D. *Out of Control Tuition*

A public, four-year college tuition has increased 213% over the past 20 years (Source: CNBC). Contrast this with the dollar's average inflation rate of 2.17% per year during this same period. It's a shocking statistic. Think a professional law degree is any different?

A few years ago, an attorney friend of mine told me that he once interviewed for an attorney position with a larger law firm who offered him $15.00 per hour here in Orange County, California. This information coincides with an American Bar Association ("ABA") Journal article entitled, "The Law School Bubble: How Student Loans Became a Threat to Your Law School's Future." Authors William D. Henderson and Rachel M. Zahorsky were spot on with "Andrea's" story about actually working as an attorney at only $20.00 per hour. Sadly, I am consulting with more law school graduates than ever before. No wonder.

According to this article, the average student loan for a law school graduate in 2010 was $98,500.00. That average now has ballooned to approximately $145,500.00. (Source: National Center for Education Statistics). So, how much money does a law school graduate need to make to pay that debt back? How long should it take to repay student loans after graduation? Assuming an average career of 20 years, the standard repayment term is 10-12 years. A bit of a recap here. We just sent our children into the fire to educate themselves at any cost, for them to spend more than half of their professional lives in debt, without the possibility of a proverbial 'parole.'

Comparing the average law school graduate student loan balance of $145,000.00 to the prospects of landing a job that would afford a standard repayment term of 10-12 years, we begin to see the problems emerge. To repay that amount of debt over the standard repayment term, the average graduate would need to gross $128,750.40. I used a single person, claiming no dependents with a standard deduction and they're income tax rate would be approximately 25%. Now where do you suppose a newly minted law school grad, who still needs to pass a background check and a bar exam, going to get that salary in their first year? In case you didn't know, these high paying jobs are reserved for the ivy league, pure bred, well-connected, wealthy. No such luck for us mere mortals. This income was obtained based on using no more that 20% of net monthly income as part of a healthy budget, to repay debt.

With an average interest rate of 6.36% for graduate loans, this graduate would pay about $51,336.28 in interest over the standard repayment period of 10 years. When we look again at the return for investment and future earning potential, a law school degree today is overpriced and a bad bet, if I were to gamble. With the odds of landing an ivy league job, likened to the odds of winning the lottery, then this graduate may never repay her loans. Unless you're a Harvard grad, then donate this book immediately to someone truly in need. Did you know that the average attorney in California makes only $40,000.00? (according to a state bar investigator)

Here's what went wrong: The institutions themselves have been paid up front to educate our future generations without any accountability for the quality or usefulness of the education delivered. Students and graduates have nowhere to go when they've been scammed out of their student loan debt for a fraudulent, overpriced, useless degree after the school is forced to close from Title IV (Appendix I Definitions) violations and greed. The federal government and the American people have been taken for a ride with our education system.

Now, there appears to be a push to privatize education altogether. In my opinion, privatization should not be attempted without accountability, inspection, reporting to the public, and a complete update using new technology.

Early 1992, the federal government became a direct lender for student loans in an effort to keep costs down. Today, our federal government is the largest lender in the world, holding more than $1.6 trillion in student loan notes on behalf of the American Taxpayers as a guarantor. The government outsources the servicing of these loans to private, for profit, companies. What this means is that when a borrower defaults on their student loans, the government allows its servicers to add 18% "collection fees," which causes balances to increase dramatically. From there, the interest compounds on the collection fees.

The federal government has traditionally played a significant role in facilitating post-secondary education, and federal loans comprise the majority of the student loan market. In addition to the Direct Loan Program and the Federal Family Education Loan (FFEL), there is also the Federal Family Education Loan Program (FFELP) and many other federal programs to fund higher education. For example, Pell grants and Perkins loans are two widely known programs that help students with exceptional need pay for college. In the 1940's the GI Bill, formally known as the Servicemen's Readjustment Act of 1944, helped 7.8 million World War II veterans receive education or training.

In 2020, while the world has faced a global pandemic, more college students were sent home to attend classes remotely. Campuses have all but shut down, while tuition was not refunded or reduced. College students now bear more burden of paying for their own utilities and internet expenses. They have had to adjust to remote learning, which creates a worse learning experience overall.

E. Families Willing to Put Everything On the Line For One Child's Education

We created a world where generations will pool their resources to send a child through college hoping to change future generations. We have wealthy families spending big money and committing fraud to get their little angels into ivy league colleges. We now have more than $1.6 trillion dollars in student loan debt in 2020. Covid-19 shut the country down in a hot second for at least two months, causing even more financial troubles for those holding student loan debt and this year's graduates have no jobs waiting for them. Parents' hopes of sending their adult children off to the university were also shocked when the pandemic boomeranged their kids back home at a time, they were excited about being "empty nesters." In 2020, many federal student loans were automatically placed into forbearance, as a result of the pandemic, but that may end before the clock hits 2021.

In the meantime, we have an entire generation fighting to become famous on any social media channel right now because the future of a college degree is less valuable than the income that fame and celebrity make from advertising deals. I would certainly not seek legal advice from a social media influencer. Certainly too, we can't all be TikTok famous.

We will continue to need doctors, dentists, lawyers, psychologists, scientists and engineers to repair and rebuild our world, keep it civil, and heal it. What we created was a system that will prevent potential future greatness for lack of money.

When someone with great potential chooses not to attend college due to lack of money, the world loses out on that human resource. We really have a human resource problem. We're already seeing corporate response to issues like education and housing. Google has pledged $1 billion to address the housing crisis in the San Francisco bay area of California. Similarly, Apple pledged $2.5 billion for affordable housing. Why? Because the billionaires need wage and hour workers and those wages are not livable wages in major cities. So now, these giants must house and probably even feed their own workforces in the future as the economic divide widens to the size of the Grand Canyon.

Have we completely lost our way in the development of our global economy? We need a basic education in financial literacy and contract law to manage our lives as adults. You must understand financial terms and basic contracts because you will sign many of them just to enter an institution of higher learning where the education is then purchased. Later, you discover that you have no job, the available jobs are minimum wage, or you have no opportunities based on some superficial label placed on you, or even the color of your skin.

F. How Can We Be Better Educated, and in the Process, Control the Consequences?

When we understand that knowledge is power, we understand that the knowledge we need in the moments where the power is grabbed. When it comes to the business of educating Americans, the power is grabbed at the front door, before you even to the hard work of the curriculum. So, we need to be better educated about the total cost of tuition and the job prospects that follow that education once completed.

Education is extremely important and we need to ensure that it remains accessible to all. Our future is dependent on leveling the playing field and opening doors so that your children can shine too. We need to learn lessons from history, rise up and become the best version of ourselves for the future. History is fast teaching us that greed and profit do not belong in education. The largest student loan servicer and second largest lender, Sallie Mae , took the entire company to Hawaii for a week-long vacation, in 2019, on the **INTEREST PAYMENTS** from your student loans. What does that tell you?

It's interesting and ironic that we're almost being forced to look at college education as to whether it's a safe bet or not. No one should ever have to gamble their life away without the possibility of wiping it away in bankruptcy. After all, our country was founded on a bankruptcy. What do you think the Boston Tea Party was all about? That's why bankruptcy is in the Constitution of the United States of

America. It's also in the Bible. We'll take a deep dive on the bankruptcy remedy in later chapter.

It appears that everything from our government starts out as a great idea. The execution of those ideas and the shaping of the agendas over time by the powerful elite, mixed in with capitalism and profit, result in the over pricing and under delivering of a quality education. The dark side of the current system is just another way we have sucked the life out of our people who seek a better life for themselves. What has happened is that those holding the power at the moment, want you to think that you have the right to pursue happiness and a better life and that the playing field is level. It is anything but level. In fact, it's rigged against you.

A professor can ruin your plans for the future with a failing grade. You could max out your student loan borrowing before completing your education and run out of money before you even finish schooling. You could get injured and be left unable to finish and get stuck repaying a loan without the benefit of a complete education. Better yet, you could have been one who got suckered into a for-profit college that promised you the moon and didn't even hit a star on your way back down to earth where the degree burnt to a crisp upon entry into the atmosphere. How can there be so many pitfalls and risks without any way out when it doesn't work out? That is the definition of a trap.

Is a college education a safe bet or not? In the midst of a global pandemic and a never-ending quarantine, we've entered a new era and our current education system is fast becoming obsolete. Our world has moved online where other giants like Google, Facebook and Microsoft battle it out for data mining and ad sales to you at the point you're about to decide anything.

The bigger question we must ask is what kind of doctor do you want if you land in the hospital? Do you want a rich doctor who could afford to go to the best university and pay his way through? Or, do you want the smartest and brightest doctor who is well-balanced in both eastern and western medicine to help heal and improve your overall health for the future? We each get to choose what we want to see in the world through our choices in studies and knowledge and whether we give it away and share it, or keep it only for the wealthy to use against the masses. Choose wisely. Future generations are counting on us today.

The best way to be better educated and thus, control the consequences of our choices is to take the time we need to gather all the facts. Research both sides of the argument and when you believe you know the truth, reverse course and research to prove yourself wrong. My gut tells me that you'll be right whichever side you choose. The only difference is that one path will likely cost you more than another. If I were to be in my son's shoes today, I believe that college is overpriced and under the Covid-19 pandemic our healthcare professionals are being stretched to the max from the ignorance and disbelief from others. Choose a degree that is well-balanced that you can take into many different sectors like a business degree, or communications for the skills needed to navigate an online world. More importantly, seek an education in the sciences, technology, arts, engineering or math. These degrees are in high demand as we move into the unknown future. Did you know there are some skills that computers will never be able to perform?

Finally, be sure to understand the total cost of the education you seek. This means understanding the total cost of tuition, books, and living expenses needed to get you through. Then, understand the available funding from free sources first like scholarships and grants. Next, look to federal loans, then private education loans. Understand the terms, the interest rates, and whether interest is deferred while you're in school or not. Let's dive deeper.

It's interesting and ironic that we're almost being forced to look at college education as to whether it's a safe bet or not.

No one should ever have to gamble their life away without the possibility of wiping it away in bankruptcy. After all, our country was founded on a bankruptcy. What do you think the Boston Tea Party was all about? That's why bankruptcy is in the Constitution of the United States of America. It's also in the Bible, Deuteronomy 5:6-7.

CHAPTER TWO

The Loan Dragon goes to College will explain Financial Aid and the FAFSA process with resources to successfully navigate that lair.

A. An Education in Student Loans and the Business of Education

No one ever thinks about the 'business' end of college. We all have a dream and a college degree is required to get us there. So, we search out the best college our SAT scores will get us into and we sign whatever papers are shoved in our faces because it's all about the goal, the dream, the degree. When you're 18 with a dream you haven't a clue what a promissory note is, or the concept of repaying the average student loan of nearly $37,000.00 with ever increasing interest rates. A college education is an investment in ourselves. Unfortunately for some, it doesn't end well.

It would be great if every parent had money available to pay for every child's college education, but that is not the norm. Better yet, what if we lived in a society where the essential worker's education cost nothing and was competitive for the brightest and best, rather than for the wealthy and those of means. Most who attend college pay at least a portion of their education by taking out student loans.

The average college student who just turned 18 years old is expected to make one of the most important lifelong financial decisions in their life, when they decide to go to college. Unless you've got enough money to bribe U.S.C. into letting your little angels in, then get in the boat.

B. Financial Aid and FAFSA®

It begins with an agreement. Your teenager will fill out a FAFSA®, which stands for, Free Application for Federal Student Aid. He or she is doomed from the very start with the word "free." There's nothing free about applying for a loan to get an education. If approved, your offspring is suddenly faced with choices and decisions about what type of loan to take: subsidized or unsubsidized (see the Appendix I, Definitions), federal or private (explanations follow). But there are lions and tiger and bears (oh my!) everywhere. So, while there are choices, how do they know which is better? They're young. But it's not just the student. This book was not intended to discuss the FREE money available for college. You'll need to go somewhere else for that. Once you've exhausted that avenue and start to take on debt, this book becomes useful.

A promissory note is a contractual obligation to repay a loan. It's one of many types of contracts that adults can enter into. The terms are dry and boring, like History class, but whether you read it or not, if you sign the agreement, you bought yourself a dragon. So, what did you really do? Here are the types of loans you may have borrowed. Since the federal government became a direct lender, all current federal student loans are either Direct Subsidized, Direct Unsubsidized, or Direct Plus.

C. Types of Education Loans

Direct Subsidized Loans are based on financial need. In this category you'll also find Perkins Loans where the school becomes the lender and Health Education Assistance Loan or 'HEAL' Loans depending upon the school and degree you seek.

Direct Unsubsidized Loans are not based on financial need. They're not credit-based, so you don't need a cosigner. Your school will determine how much you can borrow, based on the cost of attendance and how much other financial aid you're receiving.

Direct PLUS Loans are credit-based, unsubsidized federal loans for parents and graduate/professional students. Direct PLUS Loans for parents are also known as Parent PLUS Loans.

HEAL stands for "Health Education Assistance Loan". These loans were issued from 1978 to 1998 for medical students, including chiropractors. Interestingly, when a borrower defaults on these loans, the federal government revokes the borrower's ability to accept Medicare patients, which ultimate causes even more income loss and further prevents borrowers from repayment.

Perkins loans are federal student loans based on financial need. These are subsidized loans, which means that interest does not accrue while the borrower is still in school.

FFEL: Federal Family Education Loan Program (FFELP); this includes roughly 6 million borrowers. These loans were created in 1965 as part of the Higher Education Act.

Private education loans, on the other hand are either issued with a promissory note, or perhaps you signed a document that states that it is a "non-negotiable credit agreement." A private education loan is not issued or guaranteed by a government agency. This also means that you likely attended a for-profit college that was not eligible to issue federal student loans, or you exceeded the federal limits on borrowing for the out-of-control tuition for that degree.

NEW: Tuition For Work just came on the scene in recent years. We have begun to see programs whereby the local government may pay for your tuition and that tuition will be forgiven if you work for them after college. These arrangements are difficult because we humans change our minds a lot. Consider the fact that conditions change and times change. So do we. This may become another regret by being forced to work for someone to pay off debt when you just can't bring yourself to do it. Besides, most of us are already working jobs we don't like just to pay rent. To me, this is indentured servitude and another form of slavery. There, I said it. In fact, I recently came across one of these arrangements from a borrower who wanted out of the agreement because she didn't fully understand the obligations.

From the moment we are born our parents want so many things for us, including an opportunity for a better future. Wouldn't it be a better world if we fully understood the risks of taking loans out for college before we begin?

D. Resources to Navigate the Dragon's Lair

Before you read one more word. Before you deep dive into this crazy space where student loans get wiped out like a tsunami,

imagine a world where education is priceless and our survival is dependent upon the most knowledgeable of societies solving global problems as good neighbors and stewards. That would be awesome. But for now, we are going to start working so you can get where you're going and help others along the way. We are counting on you to conquer the world's problems for a happier future for all of us, but we cannot afford to have you go broke doing it!

The very first thing we absolutely must know is whether we're dealing with a federal or private student loan.

There are so many variations to this student loan dragon that you need an education in debt before you get an education that will get you out of debt. I once had a mother tell me that she couldn't understand why she owed $40,000 when she had only borrowed $20,000. You should have seen the shock when I explained what an unsubsidized federal student loan was, and the fact that this loan accrues interest from the moment the loan is taken, even though it's "deferred" with no payments due while the student is in school. Interest accrues (accumulates) from the moment you take out an unsubsidized student loan. That sucks. Did your kid know that before you sent them off to college? Did you? It's scary, isn't it! If she had known this little nugget of wisdom, she would have begun payments immediately and could have saved thousands, $20,000.00 at least. Knowing what you're getting yourself into is mandatory. The trap has been set by the very fact that a basic understanding of contract law and the terms on which the loans are based is required before even entering the institution of higher learning and there is no one to explain it to you. All I hear from you is that you were told, "If you want a degree, sign here."

All parties, especially you the consumer, need to know what you're dealing with because it will determine what options are available to you. Attorneys need to know to provide the best guidance, advice, and strategy. Here's the deal: There are different payment and legal options available, depending on the type of loan it is. I call it "sorting the thunder" because you may have more than one or two loans, and have no idea whether the loans are private or federal. But believe me, you're not alone! In fact, you're probably reading this book not only because you cannot afford the payments, but mostly because you cannot seem to find anyone to help you sort through the mess.

Bottom line, the remedies and strategies vary depending upon what type of loan(s) you have, so "sorting the thunder" is the first action step we take in working with potential clients. You need to know what type of dragon you're dealing with. For those yet to attend college, this is a primer on the different types of loans you may encounter.

E. Sorting the Thunder of Dragons

First, if you have not already done so, you should visit the National Student Loan Data System (NSLDS) website. To access this site, you must obtain a Personal Identification Number (PIN). This site also allows you to apply for additional student aid. Understanding how much is owed and what type of loan you have is the most important step in navigating the dragon's lair.

> **PRO TIP:**
> **NEVER GIVE YOUR PIN TO ANYONE.**

No one should even ask you for this number, and if they do, it's a **RED FLAG**.

Here's the benefit of logging into the NSLDS site: Any loans shown at the NSLDS site will be federal loans. We have 'sorted the thunder' at a very high level because all other loans not displayed there are private. Sorting the thunder is one of the easier steps in this whole process.

Second, pull your credit report to locate any private loans you may have. These can be found through the United States Government Federal Trade Commission (FTC). You are entitled to one free copy of your credit report every year from each of the three nationwide credit reporting companies, Equifax, Experian, and TransUnion. While the Federal Government does not control this credit report website, the link to it is on the FTC's consumer information website, and all three agencies' reports can be obtained at the same time, saving a lot of hassle.

You will only find federal student loans in the National Student Loan Data System. Register with their system to review and download all of your federal loans at this website. All other education loans will likely show up on your credit report. Knowing this information is the first step toward taming that dragon. It is important to know how many loans you have taken, the total amount owed and the various interest rates on each loan. So, how big is your dragon? Fear not the size of the dragon for the bigger they are, the slower they tend to move. All kidding aside, depending on the labyrinth path you choose will determine how much of that dragon you must eat.

F. Who Are the Players in the Student Loan Business?

Federal Players: Lender, Servicer, and Guarantor

The U.S. Department of Education oversees lenders and insurers of student loans. While the federal government does not issue private student loans, these loans are subject to preferred lender arrangements,

required disclosures to borrowers and a code of conduct must be followed for lenders issuing such loans.

a. Lender—The federal government lends money to students called, "education loans" under such programs as

Stafford (Subsidized and Unsubsidized), FFELP, Health Education Assistance Loan ("HEAL"), Perkins, Plus, Parent Plus, Grad Plus, and Consolidation loans.

b. Servicer—A loan servicer is a company that handles the billing and other services on federal student loans. The loan servicer will work with borrowers on repayment plans and loan consolidations. The U.S. Department of Education assigns the servicer after the loan amount is first disbursed.

> **ProTip**:
>
> To find out who your loan servicer is, call the Federal Student Aid Information Center (FSAIC) at:
>
> 1-800-433-3243.

c. Guarantor—Usually an agency (such as the U.S. Government for federal loans) that guarantees the loan for the government and buys the loan in the event the borrower defaults. In most promissory notes, the act of filing for bankruptcy triggers such a default, and the loan will generally pass to the guarantor during a bankruptcy proceeding.

Before July 1, 2010, guarantors were lenders. They now insure loans issued by banks. Guarantors also service loans held by the Department of Education. You may know their names: Education Credit Management Corporation (ECMC); or Connecticut Student Loan Foundation (CSLF).

The U.S. government currently reinsures certain student loans, made under the FFEL Program, against default. Guarantee agencies insure these loans directly. If a student defaults on a loan, the loan holder may submit a claim to the guarantee agency responsible for that loan. The loan holder could be a lending institution that originated the loan, or, if a particular loan has been securitized, the holder could be a trust that owns a pool of student loans. What does all this mean to you? This means that if you default on a federal student loan, the government files an insurance claim from the guarantor and that guarantor buys the loan from the federal government. In example, Educational Credit Management Corporation is a scholarship organization based in Minneapolis, MN that was founded in 1994. As of 2019 they had $370 million in revenue and $945 million in assets. ECMC provides services in support of higher education finance.

Then, there is Sallie Mae, which was a government-sponsored entity at one point, and became a private lender until July 1, 2010. Sallie Mae may service federal loans and private loans, and SLM Trusts were created to securitize many of their private student loan portfolios. Navient is a subsidiary of Sallie Mae and Sallie Mae split off its federal loan portfolio for Navient to service.

Federal loans are made under two primary programs: the William D. Ford Federal Direct Loan Program (FDLP or Direct Loan Program) and the Federal Family Education Loan Program (FFELP or FFEL Program). The Federal Health Education Assistance Loan Program (HEAL) operated from 1978 until 30 September 1998, when new HEAL loans were discontinued. Under this program, graduate students in medicine, dentistry, optometry, pharmacy, and other health fields could obtain federally guaranteed loans. Existing HEAL loans continue to be guaranteed by the Department of Health and Human Services. The types of loans available to students and key terms of those loans, such as maximum rates borrowers may be charged, are generally the same under both programs. Private lenders may charge borrowers less than the maximum rate allowed by law if they so wish. Many private lenders offer discounts and rebates to borrowers if borrowers meet certain criteria, such as making all payments on time for two years. The Department of Education also offers discounts on Direct Loans, for example, for borrowers who have payments auto-debited from their bank accounts.

Under the Direct Loan Program, which began in 1993, students borrow directly from the Department of Education. Under the FFEL Program, students obtain a federal loan from a private lender. The FFEL Program was first established under the Higher Education Act of 1965 and was known as the Guaranteed Student Loan Program until 1992.

By now, you have a global understanding of how we got here. What started as a great government idea, slowly eroded into another profit-generating machine and our world as a whole is not benefitting. Rather, there remain only a few who are holding control over the many.

Consider the position taken by some who say that they paid for their education and so should everyone else. In context, when I went to college in the 80's I graduated with an $11,000.00 student loan that was not fully paid until I bought a home and rolled it into mortgage. My income at that time was approximately $28,000.00 in the 90s. (My total student loan debt equated to 39% of my annual income for one year)

Today's graduate, on the other hand, can expect an average student loan of $37,000.00 for an undergraduate degree with an average income of approximately $59,000.00 per year. (This equates to 63% of one year's salary) This means that over the past 30 years, the cost of tuition has risen faster than the increase of income for the average graduate. This generates a greater debt burden over a longer period of time, which only gives rises to increased interest payments and profits for the likes of Sallie Mae.

G. *A quick recap.*

Getting a college education is a path out of poverty when one avoids the pitfalls and chooses an evergreen career that will endure the test of time. You must also survive global pandemics and other unforeseen events. Your college student will be required to sign a contract for an education without any guarantee of success. They know nothing about contract law until after they sign the enrollment agreements and pay for a class on contracts, only to find out it was just a chapter in a book in business class.

Then, the student is trapped into taking on more loans to complete the requirements, labs, exams, and projects that all have a cost. You're never told the total cost for the education, including tuition, books, fees, housing and interest on the debt borrowed to attend. There are no guidance counselors to explain that you have a six-month grace period after graduation, then you must have a repayment plan in place.

You're not advised what type of loans you have, or the terms. Rather, there is a pile of documents in front of you and those documents stand in the way of your future as a possibility. So, with the end in mind, you sign without knowing the full gravity of what Wonderland of a rabbit hole you just fell into. Free falling into the unknown you now must do whatever it takes to find your way out. But at what price?

Here's a chart to help you sort the thunder of dragons:

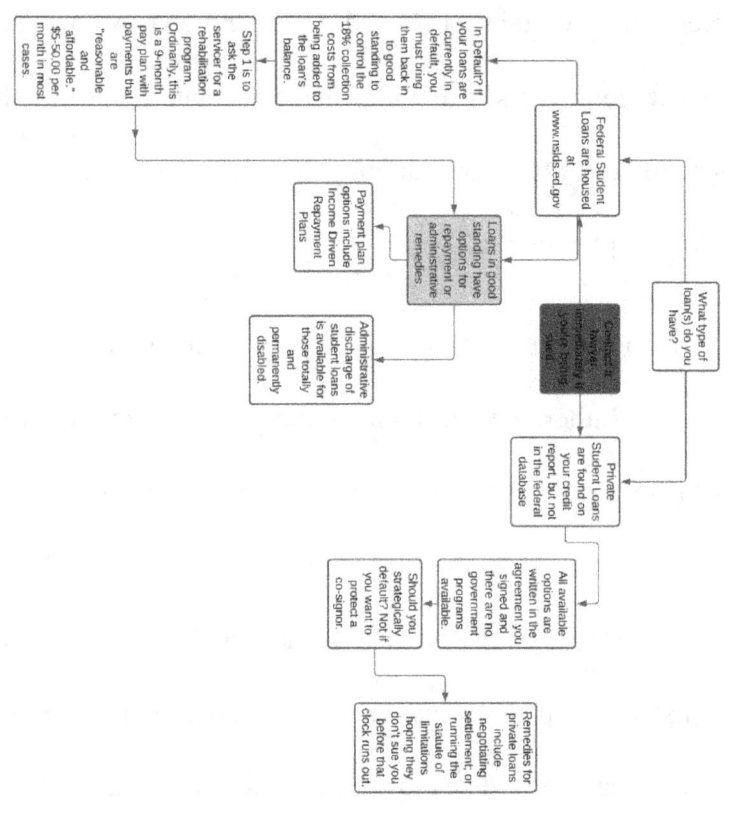

CHAPTER THREE

Taming The Federal Student Loan Dragon takes a detailed "How To" look at exploring consolidation, loan default, and alternative repayment plans.

In Chapter 1 we explored the origins of the student loan dragon. Chapter 2 described the dragons, as they come in all shapes and sizes and you learned that you needed to sort the thunder, whatever that meant. Navigating its lair has become increasingly a never-ending labyrinth.

If you have yet to attend to your higher education, go back and read Chapter 2 and seriously consider having an action plan and goal in mind before you even take the first step in completing your FAFSA.

Now that we know what kind of dragon or dragons we have, let's navigate the dragon's lair in to the world of options for taming them. Whether you just graduated, or you've been out of school forever, you must tame the dragon. In a 2019 study from New York Life, which polled 2,200 adults about their financial mistakes, the average participant reported taking 18.5 years to pay off their student loans, starting at age 26 and ending at 45.

Pro Tip for New Graduates: You will have a Grace period of six months before your first payment is due. Use this time to research your payment options and fully understand each of them before choosing your plan.

A. A Primer on Defaulted Federal Student Loan Dragons

Missing more than six months of payments will cause your federal student loans to move into default. A defaulted federal student loan is not eligible for the income sensitive repayment programs, which will be discussed later. If you have a HEAL loan, or are a healthcare professional you can lose your ability to accept and work with Medicare insured patients when your loans are in default. This makes defaulting on your student loans the worst place to be in the lair.

Defaulted loans must first be rehabilitated and brought back in to good standing. Then you, the borrower, become eligible for the other programs and remedies. Another important reason to keep those loans in good standing is that under Part 3 of the Brunner Test, which requires you make a "good faith" effort to repay your federal student loans. The Brunner Test, is the current test to determine whether repayment of your loans impose an Undue Hardship and allowing you to include them in your bankruptcy discharge. In bankruptcy, you, the debtor, must make a good faith effort to repay the student loans. While this does not require the loans NOT be in default at the time the bankruptcy case is filed, it is used as a defense by the lenders. There are a few cases in law that would say that payments made through a tax intercept is good faith, but who wants to let any problem go that far?

The consequences of defaulting on student loan debt are enormous. Even a forbearance is better than default even though seeking to stop your payments when you can't afford them is tantamount to a negative amortization mortgage. You pay nothing, paying the interest payment alone is optional and the balance owed increases. Add to that the compounding interest on the inflated balance because interest accrues on that new balance. Did you know that a baby dragon grows as long as it lives?

Loans in default that are guaranteed by the federal government can be subject to many invasive collection vehicles such as garnishing wages, intercepting tax refunds, and dipping into bank accounts to get reimbursed. The federal government doesn't require a lot of administrative paperwork to do this. It is depressingly quick.

The process begins with collection calls where the servicer can charge up to 25% in collection fees. Then, there are Federal Income Tax Return Intercepts and a Social Security offset, which includes Social Security Disability

Insurance (SSDI) but not Supplemental Security Income (SSI) and can be up to 15%, with the first $750.00 as off-limits to a garnishment. There is also a federal administrative wage garnishment *where no lawsuit is required,* that can take up to 15% of your disposable pay. According to an article in *U.S. News & World Report*, the loan holder may garnish up to 15% of your disposable pay for defaulted federal student loans. If multiple federal student loan holders are seeking wage garnishment, the total cannot exceed the lesser of 25% or the amount by which your disposable income exceeds 30 times the federal minimum wage.

B. Good Standing Never Felt So Good

Now that you fully understand the reason you need to pay attention in student loan school is to prevent default and cure it as quickly as you realize where you're at. Curing a defaulted student loan can include: 1) Settlement of the debt, 2) Consolidation of the loans, or 3) Rehabilitation.

1) Settlement of the debt

Unfortunately, the statutes only permit the debt collector to offer a 10% discount to settle the debt. The Department of Education, however, has the authority to offer a better deal. The way to get to the Department of Education is to contact the ombudsman's office directly.

2) Consolidation of the loans

One of the very first actions to take with your federal student loans is to consolidate them. A Direct Consolidation Loan will weigh the interest rates on all your loans and provide you with a single new loan, making it easier to keep track of. This also makes it easier to apply for and maintain a single loan on an income-driven repayment plan.

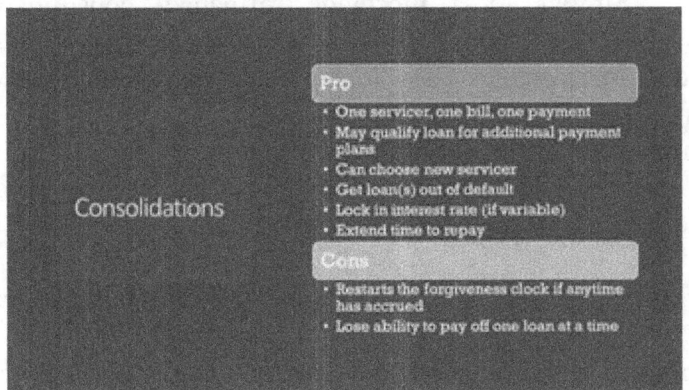

WARNING: If you have already entered into any program other than traditional repayment; i.e. Public Service Forgiveness or Income driven repayment programs, then

DO NOT CONSOLIDATE IF YOU'RE ALREADY ENROLLED IN ANY PROGRAMS. The reason is that you'll lose the time you've been in that program and be forced to start over. ***NEVER CONSOLIDATE YOUR LOANS WITH YOUR SPOUSE!*** (Divorce will not unwind a marital student loan debt consolidation loan and the federal government will not unwind it.)

Similar to a mortgage refinance, consolidating student loans creates a new loan with new terms. The process can take one to three months. However, this cannot be done when there is a wage garnishment in place. Bear in mind that consolidation for the federal loan consolidation program applies to federal loans and not private loans. (See 'Sorting the Thunder' above to be sure which of your loans are private versus federal.)

3) Curing Default Through Rehabilitation

> **Pro Tip:** You absolutely MUST KEEP YOUR FEDERAL STUDENT LOANS IN GOOD STANDING NO MATTER WHAT!

STOP! Before you read any further. If your loans are currently in default, which means that you have not made a payment in at least 6 months, then stop right now and call your loan servicer to request "Rehabilitation." Rehabilitation is a process of bringing your loans back into good standing. It takes nearly 6 months before you're considered "delinquent." Once you've fallen into delinquency, the loan servicer gets to add nearly 18%, or more, to your loan balance in collection fees. That's why default is the worst punishment for missing payments. Rehabilitation of student loans is usually the most viable remedy for a majority of borrowers. This process takes nine months with 'reasonable and affordable' monthly payments to the collector. Once the nine payments have been made, *on time*, the credit bureaus are notified that the loan is current.

Rehabilitating student loans takes them out of the default status and brings those loans back into good standing thereby preventing the problems just mentioned. The process of rehabilitation begins with a simple call to your loan servicer and requesting to rehabilitate your loans. Pursuant to the Code of Federal Regulations, the servicer will offer you a 9-month payment plan to rehabilitate your loans that is "reasonable and affordable." A $50.00 monthly payment is not uncommon. I've seen rehab payments as low as $5.00 per month and one servicer even skipped the payments altogether and placed a senior citizen directly into an income-driven plan.

Immediately following rehabilitation, the borrower can apply for an Income Based Repayment (IBR) or Income Contingent Repayment (ICR) Program to keep their loans in good standing. Regrettably, these programs are not available when the loans are in default. Once the loan is up to date, the borrower can apply for the income sensitive repayment

> **Refinancing Federal Student Loans with a Private Student Loan is a BAD IDEA**

> **Borrower Loses All Federal Student Loan Program Benefits**

> **No Forgiveness For YOU**

programs or move into bankruptcy; depending upon their goals. Curing default opens the doors to other opportunities, and this should be your primary goal. **Pro Tip:**

The key with all federal student loans is to keep them in good standing. While a forbearance may be what the loan servicer offers you on your very first call for help, that does not mean that is the solution. You must do your own research by gathering all the available information. Then, after you've read and understood your options, you can make a well-informed decision as to how best to proceed.

In addition to consolidation and rehabilitation as options for bringing these loans back in to good standing, you can always refinance these federal loans, but be warned. A refinance will take that federal loan and turn it into a private student loan. Remember that there are no repayment alternatives available for private student loans at the moment. Now that your loans are in good standing, let's explore payment plan options.

C. Alternative Payment Plans—Options for Killing the Dragon Slowly.

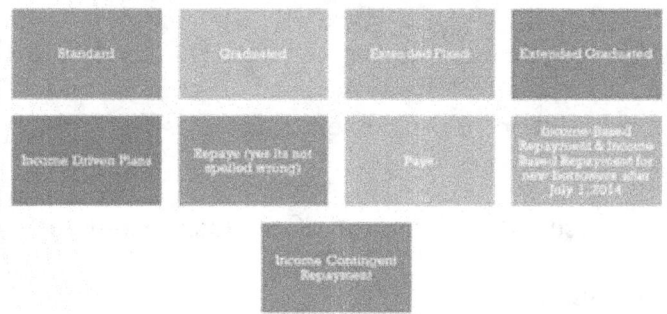

Different types of repayment plans

The Department of Education recently shared a startling figure: 57% of borrowers in an Income-Based ("IBR") and Pay-As-You-Earn ("PAYE") missed the annual deadline to update their income information. It's important for you to recertify your income and family size by the specified annual deadline. If you don't recertify your income by the deadline, the consequences vary depending on the plan.

> **Pro Tip**: These repayment plans only apply to federal student loans AND those loans MUST be on Good Standing to be eligible to these payment plans.

An income-driven repayment plan sets your monthly student loan payment at an amount that is intended to be affordable based on your income and family size.

The federal government offers four income-driven repayment plans:

- Revised Pay As You Earn Repayment Plan (REPAYE Plan)
- Pay As You Earn Repayment Plan (PAYE Plan)
- Income-Based Repayment Plan (IBR Plan)
- Income-Contingent Repayment Plan (ICR Plan)

If you'd like to repay your federal student loans under an income-driven plan, you need to fill out an application.

Here is an actual case detailing how **Income Based Repayments** can work to satisfy undue hardship. This was *In re Barrett*, No. 14-43516; Barrett v. U.S. Department of Education Direct Loan Servicing Center et al., Adv. No. 14-4161, 2016 WL 549377 (bankr. N.D. Cal. Feb. 10, 2016).

In this case, Mr. Barrett was an attorney with a spotty work history who was burdened by nearly $250,000 in student loan debt.

At age 56, he had years of negative income despite considerable effort to find employment, according to the facts of the case. Judge Novak found that Barrett "lives a spartan life," and had been driving the same car since 2003. Other facts noted by the court included: expenses exceeded income supplemented by food stamps; no assets to liquidate; no savings or retirement; and he made more than 12 years of payments on the student loans. Judge Novak wrote,

"Simply, a law degree and years of practice do not equate to a living wage," adding that, "If Barrett has been unable to establish a viable law practice after 28 years of practice, it is a fool's errand to presume that his 29th or 30th year will be any different."

As you could have guessed, the attorney for the government argued that the debtor should have instead applied for the Income-Based/Income Contingent repayment plans. The court maintained, "Given Barrett's other good-faith efforts, his failure to pursue an income-contingent repayment plan is not damming." Also remember that he did make some payments over the years. I agree that these "administrative" remedies are not required before seeking an undue hardship discharge of student loans in bankruptcy. It's a start, before coming to bankruptcy, but by no means is it a requirement for making a good faith effort to repay student loans.

Understanding how the courts interpret an individual's life circumstances in totality only serves to help you understand the bigger picture and challenges that lie ahead. This case and these facts are laid bare for you to fully grasp the importance of keeping those federal loans in good standing. I've intentionally left private student loans from this part of the discussion as they have their own chapter later.

D. Other Alternatives to Bankruptcy for Federal Student Loans

Many borrowers struggling to repay their loans are stressed out about their options because the federal government only publishes the information. Unfortunately, they have done a lousy job of making sure you're actually informed of your options.

There are some other remedies that we will explore below. When I am consulting with a prospective client for a student loan bankruptcy, I will invite them to get a hold of their federal student loans first by getting and keeping them in good standing and applying for an income-sensitive payment plan before they even file their bankruptcy case. I cannot emphasize this enough that these payment plans are the best game in town for federal student loans outside a bankruptcy discharge. Unfortunately, your federal government built the website, but failed to tell you about it.

Survival is about finding the payment plan that fits your budget, or the right application for an administrative discharge to reduce or completely eliminate what you owe. Then, setting reminders each year to follow-up and recertify your eligibility to stay in that plan until completion. This requires patience and perseverance so just know that about yourself as you take the journey of a thousand miles. Below are some remedies to research, but they are often complicated and fraught with failure. It's a good idea to seek help in understanding the latest updates and interpretation of these remedies.

These administrative remedies do not require a bankruptcy and you only need apply for forgiveness.

Total and Permanent Disability Discharge/Death

I am shocked to learn that many of you are not even aware that if you become totally and permanently disabled, then you can apply to eliminate your federal student loans.

It's called an "Administrative Hardship Discharge," and is available for borrowers who are totally and permanently disabled. It's a simple application that requires a doctor's certification for eligibility. I am informed that with a doctor's certification, you're virtually certain of an approval from the Department of Education, but I'm not one to gossip, so you did not hear that from me. Under the death certification, you'll complete an application and attach a copy of the death certificate for the borrower. Or, if you've taken out a Parent Plus loan for your child and they die, you can apply for a discharge too.

Public service loan forgiveness: A federal loan program for Direct Loans (after October 1, 2007) Requirements include:

- Must have Qualifying Employer
- Make 120 payments under IBR/ICR (No defaults permitted)
- After 10 years, the loan is forgiven and is tax free

Is it any wonder a minuscule 1% success rate exists for the Public Service Forgiveness ("PSLF") program? Established in 2007 to encourage individuals to enter and continue careers in public service by forgiving borrower's remaining federal student loan balances after they have made a least 10 years of loan payments on certain types of qualifying repayment plans while working for certain public service employers and meeting other requirements. Here's a look at the seriously ridiculous process on the path to forgiveness.

First, if you're pursuing PSLF you MUST have your loans transferred to a specific loan servicer in order to proceed. The Pennsylvania Higher Education Assistance Agency's FedLoan Servicing Unit is the exclusive servicer for borrowers pursuing PSLF or Temporary Expanded Public Service Loan Forgiveness (TEPSLF). The problems are plenty here and mainly include the misinformation about the process and how to get it right, so that after 10 years debt gets forgiven. Unfortunately, the process is not clear and here we are with only a 1% success rate. The process is initiated by sending an Email request to review and establish your place in line. You'll also need to submit an application. Did you forget something? Then, you'll go back to start until you get it right and this could take more time away from your time in the program. Even a denial can be confusing when the letters don't provide any clues as to what would be needed to become eligible, or provide what information may have been missing. The Department of Education has not fully informed borrowers about available options to contest denial decisions and this adds to the frustration. How can you make well-informed decisions without being well-informed?

Dragon taming requires you to educate yourself and constant vigilance in taming those student loan dragons. The good news is that you have options and there are resources available to you in the appendix at the back of this book.

A word about Forbearance, Deferment. What's the Difference and why do I need to know this? Simply put, deferment only applies while you're enrolled at least part-time in school. You won't see a deferment after you've left school or graduated.

In my opinion, forbearance is like purgatory. The loans just sit there and you don't need to make payments for months while interest accrues. Now, you could sit in purgatory indefinitely, if you remain eligible, or if this pandemic never ends. However, forbearance is very patient too, in that you need to continually reapply and if you don't pay attention, you could land in default, which is even worse because of those added fees and costs.

A forbearance is a request, usually made by you, to stop making payments when you experience a financial hardship. These are temporary and usually last

If you're pursuing loan forgiveness, any period of deferment or forbearance likely will not count toward your forgiveness requirements. This means you'll stop making progress toward forgiveness until you resume repayment.

So, we now know that even though the loan servicer freely offers you a forbearance every time you call them, it may not be in your best interest. I hear so often that many borrowers do not fully understand their options even though this information has been available for years and you can easily search for and find it. Even if you did find this information would be even know where to start or the right path forward for you? Well, it depends on how well you take in and manage mass amounts of information.

False Certification is an administrative remedy that is quite misunderstood.

G. A Peek Into the Future

Over at The Foundation for Research on Equal Opportunity (@FREOPP), they posted, "," an executive summary by Preston Cooper. The blueprint seems promising and provides links back to its sources for further reading. The plan proposes to target relief to borrowers who need it most; reduce the collections costs; eliminate income tax intercepts by the I.R.S., including Earned Income Tax Credit. We all agree that there is a crisis. What we don't agree on is the best option. While these are great suggestions, the poverty debt relief is already within the realm of bankruptcy. Debtors must be income-eligible to receive a discharge of their debts under Chapter 7 of the Bankruptcy Code. The Consumer Bankruptcy Reform Act of 2020 is now pending before Congress, which would include a discharge for student loans under a consolidated Chapter 10.

I agree that collections costs need to be reined in and the institutions of higher learning need to be held accountable for taking the People's money without being held accountable. Cap the interest rates and make them fixed, not variable. Setting limits on the total amount available for borrowing, may stop, or slow the colleges and universities from ridiculous and unwarranted tuition hikes. We also need control measures for book publishers in the education business, to keep them from price gouging and offer discounted E-books.

CHAPTER FOUR

Taming the Private Student Loan Dragons includes information on how to successfully navigate through collection laws, statute of limitations, Strategic default and negotiations to settle.

We separate our strategy for private student loans differently than federal loans; why? There are programs only available for federal loans as we just discussed, that do no apply for private student loans. For private student loans, you can negotiate a settlement; pay; or Fight! That's it. These loans, just like the federal counterparts, are also not dischargeable in bankruptcy without filing an adversary proceeding and proving either undue hardship; or that the loans are "not a qualified education loan." This chapter will help you navigate the private student loan industry and learn more about your rights and options to strategically deal with these pesky dragons.

A. Private Student Loans

These loans are not guaranteed by the U.S. Dept. of Education. Many remedies available under the federal programs simply do not apply to private student loans.

However, what is important to note is the difference in remedies available for these loans because they are virtually non-existent. Outside of bankruptcy, private student loan debt is treated similarly to credit card debt, which means that the statute of limitations applies on collections and the lender must sue to obtain the judgment power to levy bank accounts, garnish wages, or put liens on real property.

Brad's Story

I'm 49 years old. Back in 2003, I enrolled and attended classes at Art Institute in Santa Ana, California. I was academically disqualified and felt like I was being *discriminated against and harassed by one of the professors. I never finished my education here and I believe the school has a pattern of bad acting. I found out that in November of 2015, Art Institute through its parent corporation, Education Management Holdings II, LLC. entered into a settlement with the U.S. Government and California for allegations over the school's eligibility to issue federal and state financial aid, which prevented my school credits from being transferrable. This ultimately rendered my education useless. I'm HIV positive and the medications required to keep my condition under control are currently within my budget, but that could change any moment. I could never afford to care for my health and repay the more than $250,000.00 in private student loans that I had racked up from Art Institute. I filed for bankruptcy in 2016 and argued that my loans posed an undue hardship and perhaps that the loans were not even qualified education loans since the school had been stripped of its ability to issue federal loans.*

I eventually settled this law suit and agreed to pay $10,000.00 at 1% interest. Not a bad result for a useless education.

So, how do you know whether your loans are federal or private? It's simple. The first place you will search is the National Student Loan Data System ("NSLDS"). You'll need a PIN to gain access to this system. What will you find? This data base houses all federal student loans. So, if you have loans that you don't see listed in the NSLDS, then it's probably a private student loan. The only other place you can locate student loans would be on your credit report. If you see student loans on your credit report that are not located in the NSLDS, then you can be confident they are private student loans. See Chapter 3 for more detail.

B. Collections for Private Student Loans

Creditor collections vary between federal and private student loans. Private student loans have an important difference from Federal loans. Collecting on private loans requires a lawsuit before bank levies or garnishments can be obtained. It is important to note that outside of bankruptcy, private student loans are treated just like any other credit card debt.

What this means is that for the creditor to levy a bank account, garnish wages, or place a lien on any property, they must have a judgment in a court of law. That's right. A private student loan lender must sue you in a court of law first. So, please don't buy any idle threats from them in their efforts to collect this debt type.

For private loans, you should 1) Know about the Statue of Limitations, 2) Take time to consider a strategic default, 3) Think about negotiating a settlement even after a lawsuit, and 4) Be aware of servicing issues stemming from the Fair Debt Collection Practices Act or California's Rosenthal Act.

1) Statute of Limitations

For a private loan, the Statute of Limitations applies to the collection of this debt. The statute of limitations is a rule that sets a time limit within which a creditor may sue you for payment of a debt. The length of time that a creditor has to sue you on an unpaid debt varies from state to state. In some states, it's four years. In other states, it might be longer. The California Code of Civil Procedure §312 specifies a statute of limitations of four (4) years. Check the statute of limitations in your state.

2) Strategic Default (*Private Student Loans ONLY*)

Strategic default, where the borrower intentionally defaults on a loan in the hope of negotiating a settlement, will not save the borrower any money. Lenders never settle student loan debt when the borrower is capable of repaying the debt. However, there may be a situation where you strategically default on your loan, as follows:

Pro-Tip: This only applies to private student loans Strategically default by stopping all payments to the lender Wait several months and the lender's servicer will send letters and make phone calls to elicit payments or a payment plan.

Be sure you have cash reserves or a savings equal to no more than 50% of the debt owed because you'll likely be able to obtain a better settlement if you make a lump sum payment. If you need a payment plan, then a strategic default may not be right for you.

Important note: Each state carries its own Statute of Limitations (S.O.L.) on debt collections. This means that creditors only have a certain amount of time to file a lawsuit against you to collect on these private loans. If your state's statute of limitations has passed, then they cannot sue you to collect. The SOL date varies, too, depending on whether you signed a "contract" or "promissory note." Consult with an attorney to be clear.

3) Negotiate a Settlement Even After a Lawsuit

It's never too late to get a fresh start from debt. That is, until it's too late. Time is of the essence when a lender sues you in a court of law. Once they have a judgment, there's still time to come to some payment agreement. It's only too late when they've begun wage garnishments, or if they have executed on a bank levy.

Consumer advocates agree that it's never too late to right a wrong or get a fresh start from debt. Even if these aggressive creditors have a judgment, it's still negotiable. If they're not willing to work out an arrangement, you can always go to the court where the case was pending and ask the judge to give you a payment plan you can afford. Alternately, you can talk to a consumer attorney that understands these loans and offer other options through a bankruptcy payment plan under Chapter 13 or a discharge in full if this creates an undue hardship. (Check out the Section on Bankruptcy in Step 5.).

Terry's Story

I only borrowed $20,000.00 in private student loans for education, but my grandmother was required to co-sign with me. She ended up taking $10,000.00 of my loan for herself, but that's another story for another day. I ended up defaulting on this debt and was sued by National Collegiate Student Loan Trust.

We ended up taking the case to trial and I was amazed how little the other party's witness knew with the hard questions we were asking. At the end of the day, before the judge ruled, Ms. Kingston thought it best to talk in the hallway. I was excited that we had won, but attorney Christine told me, "Don't think for one minute that judge is going to give you a free student loan." She then proceeded to obtain an offer to settle my case for $5,000.00, when before trial, the offer was at $11,000.00. Not bad for a trial. I'm sure Christine could see the steam coming out of my ears because I would have taken that offer a long time ago. Christine took me aside and got my buy in at the $5,000.00 and I would have taken it, except that she went back and got me an actual settlement for $2,500.00 with payments of $50.00 per month until paid in full without interest! We later found out the judge would have ruled in favor of the other party for the $20,000.00 borrowed, but he would not give *them interest because the Truth in Lending Act Disclosure was never signed.*

4) Fair Debt Collection Practices Act or California's Rosenthal Act.

For a complete text of the *Federal Trade Commission (FTC) Fair Debt Collection Practices Act* of 2010, the website is From that website, you will see that

"It is the purpose of this subchapter to eliminate abusive debt collection practices by debt collectors, to ensure that those debt collectors who refrain from using abusive debt collection."

California's Rosenthal Fair Debt Collections Act extends equal protection to debtors from abusive collection practices. There may be similar laws in your state. You can find the complete California law online, but the website summarizes the intent of the law in this way: "It is the purpose of this title to prohibit debt collectors from engaging in unfair or deceptive acts or practices in the collection of consumer debts and to require debtors to act fairly in entering into and honoring such debts as specified in this title." Collection attempts that are in any way abusive or deceitful are unlawful.

If you need guidance as to what constitutes abusive tactics, you can call the California offices of Surf City Lawyers or an attorney in your state. Your student loan debts are undoubtedly weighing heavily on you and your family's well-being. You do not need badgering and bullying from bill collectors to add to your stress. However, they cannot be brushed away, either.

More recently, the California Student Loan Servicing Act (Assembly Bill 376) was passed in September, 2020 and will take effect on July 1, 2021. This new law affects student loan servicing. California will have an Ombudsman's office and authorizes the Commissioner of Business Oversight to monitor risks to consumers and gather information from the student loan servicers. They must publish their findings and make this information public. The reason for this Act is due to the student debt crisis in California. More than 3.7 million Californians owe nearly $125 billion ("$125,000,000,000.00") in student loans. On average, each borrower on average, owes $33,000.00. Defaults are on the rise and the pandemic has strained the system to its breaking point. What exacerbates the situation are the systemic predatory practices in the $1.5 trillion student loan market. You see, the longer they keep you in debt, the more interest and other predatory collection fees they take from you. It's not important whether you even pay the debt back. It's how long can they collect little chunks of money from you and stay on your family's payroll! Just like the car salesman who doesn't care how much you pay for that new car, but rather, how much you can afford to pay each month from your budget. So, if you can afford $500.00 per month for a car payment, they magically get you to that amount, after interest, a warranty you didn't ask for and oh, did you notice that your loan is seven or eight years, not five? Did you even catch that back in the 90's, student loans were designed and issued on a 10-year repayment term. Now, the "income-driven" plans take these loans out 20 to 25 years. This is what is wrong with the system when they continue to brainwash you into thinking that the ends justify the means and that if you want something bad enough, you will pay any price for it. They can go only go as far as the people will allow! We can implement more and more laws, but the conduct will not change unless the consumer takes the bull by the horns and fights back. We need to set precedent law through taking cases to appeal, as needed. Once we have case law, then we may see corrective actions taken by collectors. When predators are held to account and financially punished in an appropriate amount, an example will be set. When we have stood up and spoken truth to power and set effective protections and boundaries, only then may we see a stabilization and dissolution of the income inequality that plagues us today. California has taken these measures because the federal government, during the Trump administration, has done nothing but erase protections and has failed the American people.

4) Think Twice Before Refinancing Private Student Loans

> **ProTip:** I did not talk about refinancing in the federal student loan section because there is no way to refinance a federal loan under the current federal programs. This means that if you refinance a federal student loan, you'll be turning it into a private student loan and removing yourself from all available government remedies, including forgiveness!
>
> **DO NOT REFINANCE A FEDERAL STUDENT LOAN**

There are a lot of new players in the market to help you refinance your student loans and with interest rates at their lowest, many unwary borrowers are doing whatever they can to save themselves. That may become very costly down the road.

Private student loans have no protections or forgiveness under the current programs. That may change if Congress passes the Consumer Bankruptcy Reform Act of 2020, but until then, you need a plan. The two main reasons to refinance private student loans are to remove the co-signor(s) and the lower the interest. Refinancing your private student loans may help reduce your interest rates and that is a good thing. The only problem with that is, you may not qualify. Be sure to stay current on all your other debt obligations to maintain a credit score worthy of refinancing.

Be sure you fully understand what you're getting yourself into before you execute the loan documents and be sure all your questions are answered.

5) Litigation Strategies If You're Sued by a Private Lender

If you have fallen behind on your private student loan payments, your lender must sue you in a court of law and obtain a judgment before they have the power to garnish wages, levy bank accounts or lien your property.

READ THE COURT PAPERS CAREFULLY and then, read them again more slowly. Make a note of the date the papers were handed to you or dropped at your door because there is a clock ticking.

CALL AS MANY LAWYERS AS NEEDED TO FIND ONE THAT UNDERSTANDS YOUR ISSUES AND DISCUSSES THEIR STRATEGY WITH YOU AND QUOTES YOU THEIR FEES. You would be surprised that us lawyers have our own opinions and not all of them will get you to your goal.

A good litigation strategy is to review the facts from the borrower's viewpoint and look for legal defenses to that litigation. What I know, is that many student loans were sold off into the bond market, just like mortgages were during the 2008 crash. This means that their must be a trail of transfers and records kept at every turn. We know this did not happen and the term used in the legal community is called "standing." Standing to sue is a legal right where the creditor can show that YOU owe THEM money. We know you owe someone money, but the question is do you owe THIS creditor money? This legal defense to a private lender's law suit has proven itself to be viable where the Plaintiff lender fails to provide sufficient documentation during the discovery phase of the law suit.

Asking for documents through written discovery is a very important step to not only prepare for trial, but to put the burden on the Plaintiff to prove they even have a case worthy for trial. In my opinion lenders sue on a volume basis and expect to grab the proverbial 'low hanging fruit' with default judgments when borrowers are too broke to hire a lawyer, or fail to respond to the law suit.

When Plaintiff lenders are pressed to admit they have produced every document in their file, they often realize it's not enough to meet their burden of proof that they have the right to collect on the debt they are suing on. I have had several of these cases dismissed, that were filed by any number of the National Collegiate Student Loan Trusts, based upon their lack of documents.

As regards the National Collegiate Student Loan Trust law suits, it's important to note that they got into trouble with the Consumer Financial Protection Bureau and entered into a Consent Order where they promised not to sue anyone, unless they had the proper paper trail to prove they had standing and a right to sue. That Consent Order is useful when they "admit" that it applies to the loan in question and often leads to a dismissal after just a couple rounds of written discovery. Having a lawyer in your corner is the best defense. Having a lawyer with experience in what you need is priceless.

C. Beware of Co-Signors and Think Twice Now

Even though you may have choices when it comes to dealing with private student loans, if you have a co-signor, you need to think twice before proceeding. If you have a co-signed student loan, you can be certain that it's a private education loan. Any actions you take against your private student loans has a direct impact on your co-signor's credit too.

So, if you intend to take action, but still want to protect your co-borrower, then you may need to proceed with caution and let them know before you move. Otherwise, it's important to understand that a co-signor on a private student loans is legally obligated to pay, when you do not.

ProTip: If you intend to strategically default and you have a co-signor be sure they do not make any payments, otherwise, they will be resetting the statute of limitations clock. We'll discuss further in the next chapter.

CHAPTER FIVE

The Parent Dragon Trap explains Parent Plus Loans and co-signed private student loans which burn families who try to make college work at any and all costs.

A. Parent Plus Loans

A Parent Plus Loan is a federal student loan. The student is not legally obligated to repay this debt; only the parent/s who sign the promissory note are bound. You will never see a co-signed Parent Plus Loan. Just to be clear, see Chapter 2.

Consider This: Should You Ask Your Parents for Help? **(Hint: The answer is no!)**

Hey, mom and dad, this section is really for you. I reflect on my journey through my undergraduate degree.

I couldn't wait to move out of my parents' home, and I went to college because I didn't want to be like my mother; uneducated and divorced with three children to raise. What I didn't know is that my parents continued to claim me as a dependent on their tax returns long after I had moved out. You see, the Free Application for Federal Student Aid

("FAFSA") requires parents to submit their financial information when their children are claimed as dependents. This can either help or hurt the student's chances of being eligible for FREE grant money that NEVER has to be paid back. While claiming your kids can help you with your taxes, you might actually be preventing your kids from obtaining student loans on their own, scholarships, or that grant money. I strongly encourage parents to consider how best to help your kids get an affordable college education that will help them attain financial independence and a career they will enjoy for their lifetime.

Since my parents claimed me as a dependent for the first three years of my college life, I was ineligible for any grant money and only received $900.00 (this was 1989) in grant money my last semester in school. Besides that, they didn't pay for my college, and I was living on my own. Don't be my parents. I have a bankruptcy bias and firmly believe that kids should pay for their own education, but I'm not here to stop you from taking loans. I do want you to be well informed and make the best choices, based on your current financial ability. I am a big fan of making your kids look "poor on paper" by ceasing to claim them as a financial dependent on your income taxes and helping them to navigate an alligator-filled pond of student loans; scholarships and grants, as they make their way through the higher education realm. With that said, here are the two types of loans that I see parents take. Keep in mind the distinctions previously discussed regarding federal and private loans. Be sure to get your Ph.D. in student loans by visiting the National Consumer Law Center's website to gather all the information you need to make the best decision for yourself.

My best advice for college students currently enrolled or thinking about attending college, but haven't yet is to be sure your parents stop claiming you on their taxes as a dependent. This action may cause your parents to pay more income taxes without such a deduction, but in the long run, you'll become financially independent of your parents and that makes you eligible for more grant ("free") money for college that you won't have to pay back.

As the student loan dragon has grown, I see increasingly more parents taking on a whole new type of student loan called a Parent Plus loan, which is a federal loan. I also see nearly every private education loan being co-signed by at least one and sometimes 2 co-signors. This tells me that the lenders are looking to take down an entire family when the student is unable to pay.

I struggle with the fact that the American dream somehow obligates me, as a parent, to pay for my son's college. My parents never felt that amount of pressure and I certainly didn't have the option of having my parents pay for my college. I'm glad they didn't. I believe that our children need to learn to be independent emotionally, physically and financially so they can learn from their own choices, but it can't end there. As a parent of an adult, all I can do is support him to make the best, most sound choices for himself, given all the available information. Unfortunately, no one explains contracts or the law, let alone making our youth financially literate. What's worse is the parents who will provide for their children at any cost for their education and no one ever knows the total cost of the education being sought.

These loans are for parents only. Good news is that if your parents want to help pay for your college education and they don't have any money saved, they can happily and ignorantly go into debt for you.

Jeremy's Story

Like every other parent, I wanted what I believed was best for my children. I wanted them to go to college to have a better life for themselves. I have been a salesman for quite a while and sold precious metals. I was making close to $300k in salary, so I didn't think it would be a problem for me to pay back the more $340k in student loans to send all my kids to college. Within three years of taking on all that debt, my income began to take a drastic downturn due to the economy. At the same time my health also began deteriorating at age 67. My wife and I immediately cut our budget to the bones, including downsizing our home to reduce our housing costs by more than $2,000.00 a month.

I was diagnosed with cancer, which I have never fully recovered. Add to that, the fact that my wife is a full-blown alcoholic and I'm only now realizing it after noticing our finances were shot to oblivion. After being married for more than thirty years, you just don't abandon a partner in their time of need even if you need help too. So, I just took over all the finances to make it right.

We have nothing saved for retirement. If I ever do retire, I am only eligible for Social Security. I was approved for a Total and Permanent Disability Discharge, but I had to decline since I make above poverty wages and would not remain eligible through the three-year monitoring period.

I have asked that my student loans be included in my bankruptcy discharge, which requires I file a law suit against the Department of Education.

If you're staring at a loan application where you're the only signer, then it's likely you're looking at a Federal Parent Plus student loan. When I first started working with clients and their student loans, this is the loan I took to litigation in a bankruptcy case because this is where you do not benefit from the education. You are simply borrowing money to send your kids to college. My advice here is straightforward: Don't do take on the loan, unless you can afford to repay it yourself. Legally, your child has no obligation on this debt.

My preference is that if your child must borrow money to attend college then let them take on the debt themselves without your help. That way you're not tying a rope around your neck, but rather your child, who will be an adult by now, can learn what it means to borrow money. Of course, you can learn all you can about student loans to guide them and answer their questions. However, I find all too often that no one really knows or understands these complicated beasts. You can also give your kids money, or pay their loans as your means provide, which then makes it optional to you, not binding. Taking on debt that in all reality you cannot afford will be devastating to your retirement.

My concern is that every parent has the desire to pay for their kids' college tuition because we all want a better life for them. A better life for your kids includes understanding how money and debt works and I never learned that from my parents. Don't be like my parents. Let's guide our children instead of enabling them to think you're a bank, and they can have what they want when they want it.

B. *Refinancing Federal Parent Plus Loans to Private Loans*

New players are popping on to the market and offering a way to get control over your finances and people are buying into it, thinking it's a bargain. Unfortunately, when you take a loan out of the federal loan status and refinance that loan into a private loan, you lose any government protections and/or benefits you may have been eligible for.

Rick's Story

I was an IT professional that had worked my way through the ranks without any formal education. During the early 2000's I was making more than $300k per year in annual income. My wife and I decided to put our kids through college. So, we ended up borrowing more than $300k to put three kids through college and I didn't think that was a problem because I was making so much money. I originally took the Parent Plus federal loans.

After payments began, I was contacted by a private lending company and was offered an opportunity to refinance my loans. I thought I would be able to repay these loans within ten years, so I refinanced.

Then, it all came crashing down when I began to suffer a mental breakdown after client computers began crashing and work became overwhelming to me. My wife noticed my thoughts and actions changed dramatically and

I was talking about ending my life at one point. I ended up in the hospital for a week on a 5150 mental health hold because it was determined that I was a threat to myself and a potential harm to others. After leaving the hospital, my life is forever changed. I had to shut down my businesses and could no longer practice as an IT professional since I had no designations or formal certificates. I was diagnosed with major depression I decided to file for bankruptcy and seek a discharge for these student loans.

C. Private Co-Signed Student Loans

Co-borrowers are joint and severally (individually) liable on the debt. This means that when a son or daughter can't afford it, the co-signor (that would be the parent) has agreed to step in and pay. Here's the deal, do not sign for any loan that you are not willing to pay entirely yourself.

This means that if you're banking on little Johnnie to pay the debt and he later can't, then you must step in. Are you prepared for that? If not, then you need to say no.

When these loans go unpaid, the missed payments are reported to both borrowers' credit reports, and everyone suffers. Under the law, this is called "joint and several liability."

CHAPTER SIX

Taming through Bankruptcy answers the million-dollar question: To bankrupt or Not to Bankrupt. This chapter will take a realistic look at this option once others have been exhausted.

Would you believe there once was a time that you could file for bankruptcy and include your student loans? It's true. Student loans were dischargeable in bankruptcy prior to 1976. Before the 1970s, student loan debt was generally dischargeable in bankruptcy. Congress has gradually chipped away at student loan dischargeability since then. In 1976, it added a provision requiring proof of "undue hardship" for student loans that were less than five years old. It expanded this waiting period to seven years in 1990 and eliminated it altogether in 1998.

In the Bankruptcy Abuse Prevention and Consumer Protection Act of 2005, Congress added private student loans, which have no backing from the federal government to the list of loans that are not subject to discharge. Today, student loans are generally not included in a bankruptcy discharge, absent the debtor proving either undue hardship or that the loan is not a qualified education loan. That is how we get to the point where everyone mistakenly believes that you can't do it. Either that or you just believe what everyone tells you without doing your own research. Maybe we all need to be a bit more discerning about where we get our information.

I can take a risk in Vegas and try to make money gambling, lose, and then file bankruptcy on the debt owed. However, I cannot go to college and try to improve my life, only to somehow fail because that debt will haunt me forever.

I couldn't get out of my student loans after getting suckered into a useless degree from an overpriced institution that provided a lousy education. Oh, and let's not wait to find out about all the kickbacks given to school financial aid offices for steering our barely legal youth, with no understanding of debt, and no real-world contract law experience, into a lifetime decision that will impact their future forever!

So, where once we could discharge our student loans in bankruptcy, is now a near impossible task. It can be done.

Discharging student loans through bankruptcy first requires you to file for bankruptcy. That's a barrier unto itself with all the stigma that comes with it. Generations of shame and guilt and the helpless feeling of being a loser, or that your credit will be ruined forever. All myths by the way.

Another unfortunate fact is the stigma surrounding bankruptcy that begins with the humiliating punishment from the late 17th Century where debtors were imprisoned and considered worse that robber barrons.

Catastrophic events such as the Great Depression in the 1930's began to erode the harsh stigma and when the fear of imprisonment was abolished, the stigma began to erode. The stigma continued in the opinions of Critics in Congress, mass media, no doubt creditor attorneys, and academia, who began crying that the decline in the stigma was due to an alleged decline in morals and shame around bankruptcy, according to Efrat, n.d. Stigma was an important deterrent to bankruptcy to the critics. Unfortunately, that deterrent is very costly for consumers willing to pay a heavy price to avoid this stigma, including suicide. I believe that the stigma surrounding bankruptcy doesn't just fade when filings increase. Take the last recession of 2008 caused by the mortgage industry. Good people are forced in to filing bankruptcy when they find themselves in extreme financial hardship, which does not eliminate the stigma. Many who seek bankruptcy, continue to do so as a last resort based solely on the stigma that remains.

After filing for bankruptcy, you'll need to file what's called an adversary proceeding. You need to sue your creditors and give them an opportunity to fight like hell to get paid, while you're fighting to drop those student loans off as you exit bankruptcy court. Litigation can be an expensive and time-consuming process to get any result at all. Another major deterrent is the amount of misinformation being given by most unassuming and misinformed bankruptcy attorneys that believe student loans are not included in bankruptcy ever. That is simply untrue. There may be additional requirements to obtain a discharge of student loan debt, but it is not an absolute barrier to getting rid of them in bankruptcy.

Bankruptcy contemplates the "forgiveness" of debt. The Bible, likewise, contains debt forgiveness laws. Under U.S. law, a debtor may only receive a discharge of debts in a Chapter 7 bankruptcy once every eight (8) years. It's no coincidence that under Biblical law, the release of debts came at the end of seven (7) years.

"At the end of every seven years you shall grant a release of debts. And this is the form of the release: Every creditor who has lent anything to his neighbor shall release it; he shall not require it of his neighbor or his brother, because it is called the LORD's release" (Deuteronomy 15:1-2).

The Bible refers to debt as a type of bondage: "...the borrower is a slave to the lender" (Proverbs 22:7). Thus, the debtor is a slave to the creditor. Interestingly, the Bible declares, at the end of the sixth year, "...in the seventh year you shall let [your Hebrew slave] go free from you. And when you send him away free from you, you shall not let him go away empty-handed; but you shall supply him liberally from your flock..." (Deuteronomy 15:12-14). So, when a good plan fails, we should have a way out. After all, gambling debts are dischargeable in bankruptcy.

Ode To Bankruptcy

I don't understand why you're so attached to your credit score.
I am here to give you freedom from debt and so much more.
I can ease you from the shame and guilt.
With me, you will get financially rebuilt.
Don't sweat the threat of debt.
After your debts are gone, you'll feel better, I bet.
I know you're not a deadbeat.
I've seen your balance sheet.
You'll take a couple classes
just like the masses.
You'll also meet the trustee.
When that meeting's over,
you'll really feel free.
We might even discuss your student loans.
I'm feeling really good about eliminating debts created
from life's little clones.
When it comes to your budget,
I say let's judge it!
Put fences around your expenses and never forget how you got out of debt.

ACT: Prepare To Battle the Student Loan Dragons!

A. Student Loan Debt Can Be Discharged in Bankruptcy

When it comes to preparing for battle in bankruptcy, you must prove your case to a bankruptcy judge. Now, depending upon where you're filing for bankruptcy, meaning, what federal district you happen to live in, has some bearing on what exactly you must prove. Generally, you'll be required to prove what is called and Undue Hardship or that under the "Totality of the circumstances," you cannot repay your student loans. What most lawyers even miss is another way you can discharge student loans in bankruptcy is if the loans are, "Not a qualified education loan." Now, let's take a deeper look at these powerful dragon slaying approaches through the dark world of bankruptcy.

Undue Hardship Test; Totality of the Circumstances or the Let's Throw Spaghetti at the wall and see what sticks!

The current law requires that you, the borrower, prove that you cannot afford to repay your loans. You're asking the judge to include those student loans in that discharge order you get at the end of your bankruptcy case.

The current case law created the Brunner Test.

BRUNNER TEST REQUIREMENTS

Part 1 requires that the current financial situation cannot be conducive to maintaining a minimal standard of living during loan repayment and,

Part 2 demands that the financial situation is expected to persist during a significant portion of the loan repayment period. There must be circumstances that are beyond the debtor's reasonable control. (i.e., medical conditions; debt to income disparity; or even caring for others)

Part 3 dictates that a good faith effort at repayment must have been made,

which can include forbearance, deferment, income sensitive payment plans, and other remedies.

The Categories of Non-dischargeable Debt Under Bankruptcy Code Section 11 U.S.C. §523(a)(8). Bankruptcy Code Section 523(a)(8) outlines several categories of student debt that may be excluded from discharge. It states that a debtor is not discharged from any debt that constitutes:

(A)(i) an educational benefit overpayment or loan made, insured or guaranteed by a governmental unit, or made under any program funded in whole or in part by a governmental unit or nonprofit institution; or (ii) an obligation to repay funds received as an educational benefit, scholarship or stipend; or

(B) any other educational loan that is a qualified education loan, as defined in section 221(d)(1) of the Internal Revenue Code of 1986, incurred by a debtor who is an individual.

11 U.S.C. §§ 523(a)(8)(A)(i), 523(a)(8)(A)(ii), 523(a)(8)(B). Stated otherwise, Bankruptcy Code Section 523(a)(8)"protects four categories of educational loans from discharge."

The first and second categories of debt excluded from discharge are described in Bankruptcy Code Section 523(a)(8)(A)(i). These are "two types of educational claims: (1) educational benefit overpayments or loans made, insured, or guaranteed by a governmental unit; and (2) educational benefit overpayments or loans made under any program partially or fully funded by a governmental unit or nonprofit institution."

A third category of student debt that is excluded from discharge is described in Bankruptcy Code Section 523(a)(8)(A)(ii), and this is the focus of the Defendants' motion. This category encompasses "funds received as an educational benefit, scholarship or stipend."

And finally, Bankruptcy Code Section 523(a)(8)(B) excludes from discharge any "qualified education loan as defined in [596 B.R. 96] section 221(d)(1) of the Internal Revenue Code of 1986."

The Totality of the Circumstances, used in only a small number of districts, is the throw the spaghetti at the wall and see what sticks method, in my opinion. There have been many appellate cases since that have made this test ever increasingly burdensome. For example, part one requires the debtor prove their living a minimal standard of living, which is vague and ambiguous. This has left plenty of room for those savvy lender's attorneys to take cases on appeal for very specific issues that make it harder for you to get rid of your student loans.

After hearing hundreds of stories and handling more than thirty adversary proceedings for clients, I must say that I am discouraged with the current legal system and how it's rigged against the consumers. Education in America and the trillion-dollar student loan debt market is a fire breathing dragon that is constantly breeding and out of control. Many educated folks believe that since they've repaid their student loans that you should too. American taxpayers want individual borrowers to carry their own burden and believe that you should pay for your mistakes, but I know better. You were trapped by being misled for generations.

*Urban myth has it that if you put a **frog in a pot of boiling water** it will instantly leap out. ... But if you put it in a **pot** filled with pleasantly tepid **water** and gradually heat it, the **frog** will remain in the **water** until it boils to death.*

What happens is that you are slowly led down a path of self-destruction with one legal protection being removed at a time. Next thing you know, and nearly fifty years later, we have blatant income inequality and robber barons being exposed like never before.

Are Your Student Loans Even *"Qualified Education Loans?"*

Educational Loans and *Qualified* Educational Loans

In a court of law, categorizing the loan is very important, and can make a massive difference in the case.

Michael's Story:

Our family has had a history of drug use and abuse. When our son became a heroin addict, there wasn't anything we wouldn't do to help him. So, when the local hospital referred us to a lockdown treatment facility in Utah, we allowed our son to be sent there. He was only 17 years old at the time.

We had already exhausted all our health insurance options, so we had to take out a loan for our son's treatment. We had no idea that the Non-Negotiable Credit Agreement that we signed was going to be treated like a student loan. I had previously filed for bankruptcy and got my discharge.

Then, National Collegiate Student Loan Trust sued me in state court over this private student loan. We found Christine and are glad we did.

We moved our state court case back to bankruptcy court and filed a law suit known as an adversary proceeding against the lender. We argued that this loan was not even a qualified higher education loan. Since the loan was used for drug treatment and rehabilitation, with a small portion going toward a high school education and their child was age 17. Not one penny was used for a college education. It didn't qualify as a student loan under the law. We were granted summary judgment and the entire loan (approximately $57,000.00) was included in our discharge.

To be considered a Qualified Education Loan:

a. The debt must be incurred "by a debtor who is an individual," per 11 U.S. Code 523(a)(8)(B).

b. The debt must be "incurred solely to pay qualified higher education expenses," per 26 U.S. Code 221(d)(1) by cross-reference from 11 U.S. Code 523(a)(8)(B).

Mixed used loans, such as credit card debt or home equity loans, are not eligible, per example 6 of 26 of the Code of Federal Regulations (CFR) 1.221-1(e)(4). Even education loans are not eligible if they are incurred to pay for expenses other than qualified higher education expenses.

c. The debt must be incurred on behalf of a student who is either the debtor, the debtor's spouse, or the debtor's dependent (eligible to be claimed as an exemption on the debtor's income tax return, per 26 CFR 1.221-1(b)(2)) at the time the indebtedness was incurred, per 26 U.S. Code 221(d)(1)(A) by cross-reference from 11 U.S. Code 523(a)(8)(B).

d. The debt must be "paid or incurred within a reasonable period of time before or after the indebtedness is incurred," per 26 U.S. Code 221(d)(1)(B) by cross-reference from 11 U.S. Code 523(a)(8)(B). The regulations at 26 CFR 1.221-1(e)(3)(ii)(B) provide for a safe harbor of 90 days before or after the academic period to which the expenses relate.

It is possible that a longer period of time would still be considered reasonable based on the relevant facts and circumstances, per 26 CFR 1.221-1(e)(3)(ii), but the use of a loan to pay for a previous year's school charges would generally not qualify unless there were extenuating circumstances.

e. The debt must be "attributable to education furnished during a period during which the recipient was an eligible student," per 26 U.S. Code 221(d)(1)(C) by cross-reference from 11 U.S. Code 523(a)(8)(B).

To be eligible, the student must be enrolled at least halftime in a Title IV institution and be degree-seeking. Title IV of the Higher Education Act of 1965 (HEA) covers the administration of the United States federal student financial aid programs. Study abroad is only eligible to the extent that it is approved for credit by the home institution.

Approval requires a two-tiered analysis:

1) Whether a debt is an educational "loan" and, if it is, then

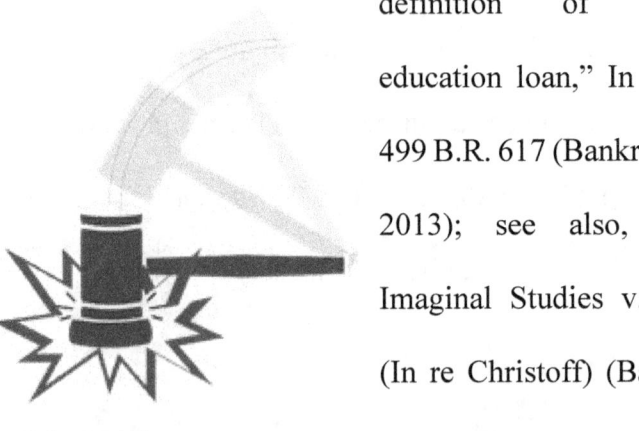

2) Whether it meets the Internal Revenue Code definition of "qualified education loan," In re Oliver, 499 B.R. 617 (Bankr. S.D. Ind., 2013); see also, Inst. of Imaginal Studies v. Christoff (In re Christoff) (Bankr. N.D. Cal., 2014).

An eligible educational institution is that which is described as qualified to participate in a program under Title IV of the Higher Education Act of 1965, as amended. 26 U.S. Code §25A(f)(2). Wills v. Sallie Mae; (Bankruptcy Court S. D. Ind. 4-23-2010; Case #08-80404, Adversary Proceeding #08-58043; decision April 23, 2010).

Judge Grossman, in the case citation "In re Wills" concluded that since Congress specifically mentioned loans in Subsection 523(a)(8)(A)(i), but not in 523(a)(8)(A)(ii), it intended to refer only to conditional stipends, veteran benefits, and other cash-benefit programs that are distinct from traditional student loans and therefore found that Decena's loans satisfied this Section.

Did you know? Private Student Loans For Unaccredited Schools are NOT Considered Student Debt in Bankruptcy?

After I've talked about how hard it seems to get rid of these pesky dragons, I present to you, an entirely unique dragon. The dragon that actually dies in bankruptcy. This dragon actually gets included in your bankruptcy discharge WITHOUT all those tests, burdens and law suits. Oh My!

How To Tell If You're School Was Accredited

There are important distinctions between accredited and unaccredited schools. If you are not sure if you have attended an unaccredited school, you can check on the Council for Higher Education Accreditation. Another way to check is a simple Google search using the terms, "Federal School Codes List" You need to first locate the school you attended, followed by the school year you attended. Once there you'll see the entire spreadsheet of accredited schools. If you find your school on the Federal School Codes List, then it was accredited at the time you attended, and you would NOT be eligible to discharge your education loans under this section of the Bankruptcy Code. Don't worry, you may still be able to prove an undue hardship.

It is usually best to go to an accredited school (accreditation means the school has met and is maintaining a modicum level of standards set by the accrediting agency).

In the April 2016 case *IN RE* Decena, the woman debtor named Lorelei Decena was *ineligible to sit* for the medical boards in multiple states in the U.S. because the medical school she had attended (St. Christopher's college of medicine in Senegal, Africa) was not an accredited medical school. After all the work and all the money, she was not allowed even to take the boards in the United States, much less try to pass them. In the case, the judge determined that the debtor attended an unlicensed and unaccredited medical school not found on the Federal School Codes List for the school year attended.

It might be easier to get into an unaccredited school, but it may not be worth the expense.

The good news? If you *do* have to file bankruptcy—a last resort but sometimes the only answer—the loan or loans that are taken out for an *unaccredited* school's expenses can be treated differently than a student loan and can be included in the bankruptcy discharge. Why? Because if the school is unaccredited, the courts do not regard the loan as a *bona fide* student loan.

However, if your school is NOT on the list, then it might be worth exploring your bankruptcy option to discharge your legal obligation to repay that debt. To make triple sure, you can go to the school's website, and they will usually have a link telling you the year of accreditation, the accreditation organization, and when the next accreditation will occur.

Unaccredited Schools Outside the United States

As in the case of Ms. Decena above, many unaccredited international schools will gladly take your money. The United States Department of Education officially calls these schools diploma mills, as you can see from the link's name in the footnotes. From their website, you will see tips from the Better Business Bureau that suggest red flags for unaccredited schools. Also, the same Department of Education website advises you to be aware of

- *Fake accrediting agencies*
- *Foreign accrediting that is not recognized by the Secretary of Education*
- *Fake credential evaluation services*
- *College credits offered based on life experiences*

Also be mindful that ".edu" internet addresses may not be legitimate, and that scholarship and financial aid scams are everywhere. The Federal Trade Commission provides information on ways to avoid these scams.

While it might seem that some of these topics are outside the scope of freedom from student loan debt, it's all related. If you give money to the wrong people, that's less money to pay your student loans, and you are facing the extra bother of paying for an education that will not serve you.

Specialists in our field are seeing that U.S. students have attended unaccredited schools are carrying an enormous amount of student debt. The terrible news is that sometimes employers disregard an education from an unaccredited school—making it even harder to get a job to pay off the student loans. It's hard to get a job when no one takes your degree seriously.

It's difficult enough to get up and go to work some days. It's harder to get up and go work when you're desperate and depressed, that brings on anxiety. These are the student loan dragon's cousins. When life's debts become unduly burdensome, an undue hardship, and a life sentence; we take on feelings of shame, guilt and might even believe we're somehow "not good enough." These are dragons too. The most important tool you need right now is courage to battle the dragon and the others that follow it. Every day you wake up, you have a choice. You are not weak because you can choose today.

Choose hope. Seek knowledge and information both good and bad. Take the time you need to make an educated and well-informed decision for yourself. Learn to tame the dragon and get control. If you're in overwhelming debt right now, recognize that and the fact that you're about to go in to battle against that burdensome creature.

If you're feeling as though you're the walking dead, or that things won't ever be the same again, it is my mission to empower you with the tools and weapons you'll need to battle your student loan dragon, which will likely pour over into the rest of your life.

B. The Future of Student Loans in Bankruptcy

Currently, student loans in bankruptcy still require an adversary proceeding (a lawsuit) in which the debtors must ask the bankruptcy court to order their student debt obligations discharged in bankruptcy. Otherwise, they will not be included in the bankruptcy discharge.

Finding a qualified bankruptcy lawyer that understands the Rules of Bankruptcy Procedure and litigation will prove more difficult. The reason is that getting a bankruptcy discharge requires litigation, and that is a completely unique skill set, above and beyond simply helping clients file for bankruptcy protection. This means that not only will consumers be required to file a bankruptcy case; they will need to file a lawsuit against their creditors and ask the court to determine each student debt obligation to be discharged.

Don't be discouraged if the institution where you studied is accredited because there is still the Undue Hardship bankruptcy discharge that no longer requires a medical condition to satisfy. Some, but not all, courts use the Brunner test, as above, to determine undue hardship. Some use the "Totality of the Circumstances" Test or the Health Education Assistance Loans (HEAL) test. It varies by jurisdiction, and a local bankruptcy attorney can guide you.

Unless you've been living under a rock these days, you've seen our presidential candidates starting to promise student loan forgiveness of some sort. It's as if we're all back in high school and the student body president promises pizza lunches if you vote for them. The better news is that we currently have a bill moving through Congress called the Student Loan Repayment Assistance Act of 2019 (H.R. 655)

As recently as June 25, 2019, the National Association of Consumer Bankruptcy Attorneys was given the opportunity to testify before the House Judiciary Subcommittee on Antitrust, Commercial and Administrative Law during the hearing "Oversight of Bankruptcy Law and Legislative Proposals" and made a strong call to restore the bankruptcy discharge for student loans. Now wouldn't that be a great achievement. That bill is H.R. 2366 is now pending before Congress.

Our goal is to help our clients repay their student loans to the best of their ability. If that is not possible, we aim to work with them so they can discharge their student loans and begin to live a life without the stress of late payments, bullying creditors, higher interest rates on any future loans, and the possibility of being denied employment because of unpaid debts. I'm giving you the strategies and tactics to battle the student loan dragons.

The Cares Act became effective March 27, 2020 as a response to the Covid-19 pandemic. This provided for a forbearance and interest waiver for all Direct Loans owned by the federal government. Older Federal Family Education Loans ("FFEL") were not protected by the Act, but the Department of Education encouraged servicers of these federal loans to take similar actions to relieve borrowers of the need to make payments during the pandemic. Those with Perkins loans or private loans also were not protected from interest accrual or the need to make payments and this resulted in a patchwork of forbearances and other temporary payment relief. Keep in the mind, the rules you learned about forbearance and how it's a holding place. The only light in this tunnel is the fact that interest is frozen for the time being.

The CARES Act provided other relief such as no need to recertify income during the forbearance period, suspension of all ongoing collection activities, and for credit reporting purposes, any payment that was suspended would be treated as if the borrower made a regularly scheduled payment. President Trump extended the CARES Act as it related to student loans until the December 31, 2020.

ProTip: *Pull your credit reports to see how your student loan servicer has been reporting your account to the credit bureaus. Be sure to obtain regular statements that show no change to the balance due during this time frame as well.*

The Biden Administration brings hope and fuel to the student loan debt crisis that continues to loom. There are talks about wiping about small amounts of student loans in the Biden camp, but no decision has been made. Unfortunately, wiping out a small portion of debt would be helpful to only a few. I see hope for our future, but we have a long road ahead. The cancellation of student loans needs to come with a change in lending practices. Colleges and universities need to be held accountable for the education they provide on the People's dime. We need to unify on this matter for the greater good and future of our country because education is core to our success.

The bankruptcy system is broken for student loans. House Judiciary Committee Chairman Jerry Nadler (D-NY) and Sen. Elizabeth Warren (D-MA) on Wednesday, December 9, 2020, introduced the 'Consumer Bankruptcy Reform Act of 2020,' which proposes to replace the current systems of chapter 7 and chapter 13 personal bankruptcies with one system, chapter 10, in addition to specifically addressing the eligibility of student loans for discharge in bankruptcy.

The purpose of the Act is to establish a bankruptcy system that helps individuals and families in the United States regain financial stability and protects against abusive and predatory behavior by

1. Streamlining the process of filing for bankruptcy, simplifying court procedures in bankruptcy, and

lowering the cost of bankruptcy for both consumers and creditors;

2. Creating a single-chapter consumer bankruptcy system that allows consumers greater flexibility in addressing their debts and prevents disparate treatment of similarly situated consumers;

3. Offering consumers more and better options to deal with their debt, while ensuring fair treatment of creditors;

4. Making it easier for consumers to pay an attorney for counsel or representation in a bankruptcy case;

5. Simplifying the identification and treatment of cases by expanding the number of routine cases that are handled by the court in which there is no chance of a reasonable payment to creditors and reducing paperwork requirements in those routine cases;

6. Allowing modifications of car loans based on the market value of a car;

7. Allowing the discharge of student loan debt on equal terms with most other types of debt;

8. Reducing racial, gender, and other harmful disparities in the availability, accessibility, costs, and outcomes with respect to the bankruptcy process;

9. Ensuring the fair treatment of claimants for domestic support obligations;

10. Reducing abusive creditor behavior; and

11. Closing bankruptcy loopholes that allow the wealthy to exploit the bankruptcy process.

Well now, if this is not the best Holiday Gift Basket of an Act, I don't know what is!!! If my reading of this Act is correct, consumer debtors will be able to file a bankruptcy case every Six (6) years instead of the current Eight (8) year waiting period. It eliminates the requirement to file an adversary proceeding to include student loans in that discharge, which has been the greatest barrier to a fresh start for many debtors. With that said, help is on the way. Hold tight and keep those loans in good standing, at any cost. It wouldn't hurt to call on Congress to pass this bill.

Current Trends for 2021—These are strong possibilities, but are NOT CURRENT LAW AS OF THE PUBLISHING DATE OF THIS BOOK

The first, is a possible immediate forgiveness of $10,000.00, a policy under H.R. 6800

Next, the Biden administration is also looking into a remand of the current forgiveness options, currently known as "Income-Driven Repayment" plans. This would lower payments from 10% of discretionary income to 5% and a waiver of the tax consequences from the cancelled debt at the end of these programs.

Third, there may be a more enticing Public Service Forgiveness Program for public sector workers like teachers, military and non-profit workers. With a 99% fail rate under the Trump administration, we should see a higher approval rate for pending applications. This forgiveness program looks ripe for consumers to achieve some success. It's time to re-apply and put your name back in the hat to see if the answer changes.

The Consumer Bankruptcy Reform Act of 2020—will include student loans in the bankruptcy discharge. There are a host of other laws pending and too numerous to name. Just you try to keep an eye on this moving target of student loan forgiveness.

CHAPTER SEVEN

Dragon Birth Control (hahahaha) This Chapter is especially important for anyone who has not yet signed on the dotted line, with valuable "what to look for" tips.

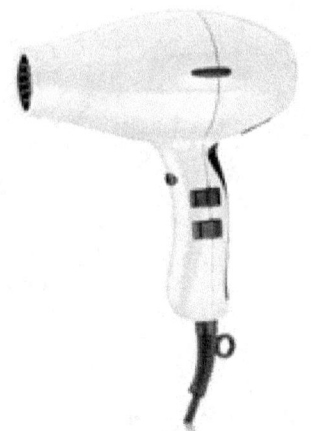
Do you know who the smartest person in the room is? The smartest person in the room is my hairdresser. She never went to college. She knew what she wanted to be at a very young age. She went straight to cosmetology school, graduated and got to work in a salon. I don't even know the cost of cosmetology school, but my quick internet search tells me, on average, cosmetology school costs anywhere between $5,000 and $15,000 to attend.

She soon got her cosmetology certificate and her license and became a hairdresser while still in her 20's. She charges more than $200.00 every time I see her and I can imagine that she's able to handle at least six to seven cuts per day. That is $1200 per day on a good day. Take that out for a whole year and she's likely making maybe $288,000 per year gross revenue for her small business. Think back to the average income for attorneys in California and what my hairdresser is likely making and you may become sick to your stomach.

How's that for someone who didn't go to college? Add to that the fact that she doesn't have to pay back student loans, has no debt, and shares an apartment with some friends to keep our costs down.

Her small business is being run in a room within a bigger office suite, sharing space with a massage therapist, a manicurist and list of other specialties, so it works like a mini spa where she's working at and it's beautiful.

Whatever happened to the trade jobs and becoming a master carpenter, woodworker, a tile layer, or construction worker, or a journeyman and those jobs? We still need manufacturing and there will always be a need for skilled labor. We still need things to be made and there are other ways to contribute to society other than with a college education.

Reading books, too, never hurt anyone —like this book, for instance.

A. Before You enroll College

Have a Plan. Creating your plan for your future requires you imagine yourself doing your life's work, or doing a job you think you would really enjoy. During law school, I remember a classmate who had always wanted to be a public defender when she became a lawyer. She graduated from law school and passed the bar exam on her first attempt. She even landed her dream job only later to discover she hated it. Don't take the road less travelled only to end up in regret. Get to know yourself first. Work with your strengths and educate to compensate for your weaknesses. For example, when I have a project and I'm not sure about the entire process, I'll consult with several online sources and watch some videos to educate myself and see my project from several different viewpoints before taking my first steps.

Consider taking personality tests and discovering as much as you can about yourself and your own natural talents. Then, choose a career that matches with those natural talents and I bet your life will go much further. Just like my hairdresser, when you know, you just know. Learn as much as you can about the daily activities that are performed for the type of career you're drawn to. Don't discount life events that land you in a completely different place than you had originally intended. Learn to be flexible and let go of the outcome in terms of not getting what you want. Don't push yourself to go to college, if it's not something you truly desire because there are so many possibilities to make a livable wage or even become wealthy.

In high school, I had always wanted to be a nurse, but my grades were average for science class and I was concerned that I might not make it as a nurse. My grandmother was a nurse. During my junior year, I had taken a speech class instead of another English class. We actually had to give a speech in that class and I will never forget my first experience at the podium. Butterflies in the pit of my stomach as the adrenaline rush flowed through my veins. I braced the podium so it would hold me up if I fainted. I delivered that speech and aced that class. I fell in love.

The **BEST ADVICE** I ever received: *My speech teacher told me to do what I love and do what comes naturally and the money will follow.*

She was right. It took me longer than expected and I've taken a very unconventional route to get where I am today. I went to college because I didn't want to be like my mother, a single mom raising three babies as a supermarket cashier.

It requires work, discipline, dedication and being able to focus intently on a goal until it arrives. I am the first member of my immediate family to have obtained a college degree. Add to that a Juris Doctorate degree as well. Recently, I've taken to looking back at my family history and learned that some of my Irish ancestors were lawyers. I was excited to learn more about my family's lineage and I've gained incredible insights. It seems I am simply a new and improved version and next generation for my family. So, before you enroll and volunteer to endure the gauntlet while trying not to get trapped, take some time to consider the best route for you.

Consider a career that doesn't require a college degree. The trades are jobs where you work with your hands. Welders, plumbers and electricians will always be in demand. Add underwater to a welder's job and the price jumps.

In the future, we need to counsel our young people to research and think carefully before taking on substantial educational loans. Consider choosing a degree that will pay the bills, and to beware of the unfortunate pitfalls associated with unaccredited schools, scams, and complete misrepresentations in the area of higher education.

B. Tips for Keeping College Costs Down

Live at home. I know. I know. Worst tip ever, but it's the best thing for saving. Deal with it. Don't change degree choices in the middle of your education either. Changing your major can be expensive. You'll be required to take more classes and that costs both time and money, so choose wisely before you even enroll and stick it through.

Still, there was an embarrassing secret I wrote about then but never published, nor did I try, because I was ashamed of my contribution to a national debt now soaring over $1.6 trillion — a burden I took on in exchange for the opportunities of generational progress and financial stability, and the privilege of career fulfillment.

C. Don't Piss Off the Teachers

Seriously. We all have to deal with difficult people in life. After the 2020 election it has become even more clear how much hate and anger are out there. So, for better or worse, we need to learn to get to our goals in spite of these barriers. Consider a difficult teacher or professor (if they deserve the title) and opportunity for you to level up your people skills. I love the YouTube "University" for free online videos that so many of us professionals put out for business generation that you could practically get a degree simply by watching videos. In fact, you can get an entire degree in learning how to deal with people by taking a degree in speech communications. That's a life skill that will open many doors and will work in every industry and job you'll ever do.

Stay focused on your goal and steer clear of the barriers to your own success. Be like water and flow over, under and around rocks that sit in your path. This is one of the best ways to keep your overall costs down. This may require you to bend and grow in ways you never initially dreamed of. Just keep in mind that these people are your greatest teachers in life. Learning to deal with challenges brings more opportunities to grow and learn about yourself and the world around you. Pay attention to the details. Think independently and for yourself. Then, look at these difficult moments from as many different points of view as possible to see it from every angle. Take the multiple perspectives and boil them down into a single decision. Then ask yourself, are you motivated by love or fear? Don't move if your decision is fear based. Only move when you're moved by love. This too, is a skill that must be learned to effectively navigate life that you may not be taught in any school.

D. Avoid Scams and Bribes

As the economic disparity between the extreme haves and the rest of the 90% widens, there will be a continuing rise in online scams, and fraud that you need to protect yourself every step of the way. This includes companies that promise to help you with those student loans, or help you get into college. Back in my day in the late '80s, I knew that I had six months grace period to figure out how to repay my loans. We all knew how to consolidate our loans, too. What I can't seem to figure out is how all these companies cropped up, promising to help you do something that you should know how to do and could easily do for yourself. Listen, I know you spent a lot of time studying the subject matter that you sought a degree in, but part of the process is also learning how to navigate the education system of enrollment and payment for that education as well. Always ask questions and be sure to fully understand what you're signing, or you probably shouldn't do it. Don't get caught up in the glitter and glory; be practical.

When I was graduated from college, there weren't any companies that I could hire to help me "consolidate" my loans; we just did it ourselves. Listen, you got an education and I hope it taught you to be resourceful. You have the internet for crying out loud. Take advantage of the resources provided here, because I provide this information to everyone I consult with. It's all covered here.

Just because you're in debt, doesn't mean you have to be taken advantage of on the way out of debt. If I haven't mentioned this before, I'll say it again. The brain gets scrambled when you're in debt because you're under an enormous amount of stress, even fear and anxiety might hop on the stress train. Take time to breath and let your mind wander. Taking time includes what I call "making soup." Like our grandmothers would take all the ingredients for soup and throw them into a large pot to boil. For hours. Just as you would make soup, you take time to gather all the information you can from multiple sources and simmer for hours or days if necessary. Then, in that time, the answers usually show up.

Taking responsibility for your life; where you stand now is where your power lies. Once you realize that you got yourself here, then you will know you have the power to solve your own problem. When we blame others, we are powerless to change our own circumstances.

BE CAREFUL OF SCAMS!

It's a Scam….

1. If they ask for an upfront fee to help you

2. If they ask for your personal information, i.e., social security number, or Personal Identification Number (PIN) for your National Student Loan Data System file;

3. If you're talking to a salesperson who is pressuring you to sign up for their service before you know what they will do for you;

4. If they promise immediate loan forgiveness, which doesn't exist

5. If it sounds too good to be true.

Remember: Never pay money up front for any help with your student loans. Advance-fee scams are great because they get your money *before they have to do anything!* You should never have to pay money to get money *whether it's* for a consolidation or refinanc*ing* of your loans.

While it's good advice to consolidate your student loans right after you graduate, there are consolidation loan scams where they take your money and nothing gets done, or you're sold on a consolidation after you've had some of your loans in an income driven repayment plan, only to find out you now lose your time served in that program and must start over because a consolidated loan is now a new loan.

Law firm scams claiming to be able to settle your student loans. The problem is they can't help you with your federal student loans and their best advice in settling the private student loans is to stop making payments and go into default first. This strategy causes your credit score to get trashed, but these firms won't tell you that. They make an incredible sales pitch by reminding you that you can't include student loans in bankruptcy, making them your only option. This is simply not true.

Anyone promising to get rid of your student loans is likely a scam. Lawyers' code of ethics prevents us from promising or guaranteeing an outcome. Since we're held to a higher standard and have no magical powers to make such promises, then it would seem fitting that a financial firm has no greater powers than a lawyer.

The worst offense ever is when your student loan servicer, an entity you're supposed to be able to trust with good information, steers you into a forbearance, rather than sharing other income driven repayment options. That, friends, is a scam.

Be especially wary if you're asked to share sensitive personal information.

Be suspicious if the company advertises on social media or shows up in search engine ads.

Listen, I know you're in desperate times, but it doesn't mean you need to take desperate measures by adding more scams on the way out the door.

E. Questions to ask any professional before hiring them

- What is your experience in handling student loans?
- What can you do to help me with my student loans?
- What are your fees for this service you just mentioned?
- What other costs can I expect?
- What other options do I have?
- Why should I hire you?

CHAPTER EIGHT

The Tail/Tale So What? Why it matters. In Conclusion What do tame dragons eat?

Influencers and media continually telling the public that student loans cannot be discharged in bankruptcy is an absolute misnomer, but it's not easy either!

The perpetual debt machine and overburdening of future generations cannot be maintained indefinitely. While federal student loans have many programs, those programs come with confusion, frustration and high failure rates. In bankruptcy, currently you must sue the lenders and ask the judge to include your student loans in your bankruptcy discharge. This process is litigation, which we call an *adversary proceeding* in bankruptcy.

A. Why it Matters?

The student loan debt crisis matters because it's a major symptom among other major symptoms that are draining the very life out of the entire World. It's 2021 at the time of this writing and this crisis exposes the racism and income inequality among the few at the top, while the majority of Americans scrape for a living wage.

It matters what kids are taught in our schools and whether or not we are globally competitive in education. We need education for the changes needed in this new, post-pandemic world. It matters that our government, as public servants, have a duty and obligation to inform the public and tell the truth to the American People. Fairness and equality matter and that's why this topic is crucial.

When we educate for the future, we can create an even brighter world. One that is sustainable and provides for everyone, equally. We want the brightest doctors, scientists and engineers to save us and keep us safe from harm. It matters because we want a better future for our children without being enslaved to debt for all eternity.

Tough choices are looming in the wake of the Covid-19 pandemic that has taken the economy and many small businesses with it. The issue of student loan debt that nearly 43 million Americans are burdened with, needs to be addressed.

B. *Truth over Stigma*

If I told you that I have filed for bankruptcy, would you believe me? It's true. So have many major corporations and some famous people you might recognize. Dave Ramsey has filed for bankruptcy; so has Walt Disney before he created Disneyland. What these people all have in common is, they eliminated their debts quickly and then launched their money-making ideas to create their empires. Stay curious and open to multiple perspectives because you're in control over your life and no one else can live your life, but you.

It's high time you realized we've all been duped into thinking that we need an overpriced education so we can work for the likes of Microsoft, or Amazon, when any one of us can be the next major player in the market. The education we need is to learn to think independently for ourselves.

C. *The Bigger Picture*

In looking back in history, we discover how we got to where we are today. The reality of today provides huge financial gains to a very small group of companies owned by even less of us and they want to keep it that way. You see, if you really knew what they know, you would be outraged.

The future of our planet requires that we trust our scientists, follow doctor's orders, and take advice from our lawyers and therapists. Trust is required, but it's been eroded by false promises of a better life and every time we seem to get ahead, the rug gets pulled out from under us and the goal posts are constantly being moved. It's never ending. Instead, our country is acting like immature elementary school children fighting over a swing set.

We need educated citizens because knowledge is power. If we want to be the most powerful country in the world, we need our citizens to know what is going on. The United States is not number one in education. In fact, it was during law school that I learned that the average person has only a seventh-grade level of education.

But what, exactly is "education?" Certainly, we will continue to need to know the basics to navigate life like using smartphones, microwaves and Alexa, but what about making money, managing it, and avoiding getting scammed out of your future? What if we all simply treated one another in a fair and equitable manner from the beginning, thus eliminating the scammers all together? What if?

D. Morality and The Price of Education

How we got here was set in motion a long time ago when the likes of Sallie Mae set out to make it harder for college graduates to get out of their student loan debts in bankruptcy. Once the lenders were safe from a bankruptcy discharge, they feasted on their newfound wealth through exploitation. The student loan dragon hoards shiny money and will continue to collect indefinitely, until they can collect no more. These dragons do not intend to completely destroy the economy, but they just cannot help themselves from their greed. Sadly, if you seek the benefits ordinarily brought by a college education, currently, you're stuck with the bill, no matter to cost, forever. In Chapter 1, we were shocked to learn that the costs of a college education have skyrocketed more than 213% in the past twenty years. We have not seen salaries or cost of living increases that would justify such an increase. So, how do you sit there, telling our overburdened college graduates to just "suck-it-up" and pay the price when our price was much lower as compared to our cost of living?

As a consumer bankruptcy attorney, I've heard thousands of stories and the majority of you believe you have a moral obligation to repay your debts. You believe that by doing so, you're honoring your contracts. I respect that. However, I would assert that when your back is against the wall, would you agree that a little help would go a long way toward keeping you from becoming homeless? What if I told you that you were scammed? Do you believe that you still have a moral obligation to repay a debt that was created from fraud? Consider the perspective that many college graduates had no idea what the total cost of their education was, or whether their parents might be taking on too much debt for their four years of freedom and exploration. Families are willing to put generations of wealth on the table for the possibility that one of their own would do better in the world.

On the other hand, you have the likes of private market lenders and loan servicers, collecting eighteen percent of the loan balance for defaulting student loans. These same players are all too happy to place your loans in forbearance; or a place I like to call "purgatory." There are no payments in a forbearance, but interest continues to accrue and that's how they get paid. The more interest you pay, the more they make. Sallie Mae took their entire company to Hawaii for a week, solely on the interest they collected. So far, we have families willing to do whatever it takes for a college education; and, we have collectors taking advantage of a situation based on the difficulties in discharging student loans in bankruptcy.

Finally, you have a perfect circle when you add in the colleges, universities and institutions of higher learning. They set up their admissions offices that are more akin to a boiler room, sweat shop profit machine. Currently, they have no obligation to contribute to the losses that the

American taxpayers may have to bear when the borrowers default and cannot repay these loans. The game the student loan dragon plays is thus; collect shiny money from you for as long as they can without destroying you, and do it for as long as they can. Once you break, they write off the debt and the American people take the loss.

Where is the morality of creating a unity of our states for the betterment of us all? Education is the foundation for our future. Today's children are tomorrow's leaders and we need to prepare them mentally, physically, emotionally, creatively, and Spiritually, as possible. We need our religious leaders to all join forces and create a joint mandate for a foundation for living such as treating everyone as you would treat yourself. This may be the beginning, if we would all commit to being open to new possibilities for a way forward as a whole.

When we have a need for healthcare workers, we should seek comfort in knowing that we have citizens ready and educated to help. I also want to mention again that we need the best and the brightest people to step in to these jobs and it is my belief that we're wasting human resources when money is the barrier to success. We don't stand a chance when we choke out the 99%. Perhaps the current broken system was designed that way.

As colleges and universities continue to shutter from the 2020 Covid-19 pandemic, they will be forced to adapt and adjust to the future of online degrees and education. They will be required to make price adjustments for these changes and learn to live on less income for executives; less pool tables. Reforms are looming from including student loan debt in bankruptcy to holding institutions of higher learning accountable for their failures in educating and overcharging the America taxpayers. We must force conditions on the funds received from our government;

including strengthening academic freedom when federal funds are tied to a willingness to adopt changes.

E. The Future of Education Must Transform

The future of the world will depend upon those with specific skills and knowledge to take up leadership roles and actually lead. The skills needed for us are not new. However, we will need to change the subjects currently being taught in our antiquated school system. But how do you overthrow a social institution that has gone off the rails? VOTE and spend elsewhere.

Obviously, we need to teach technology, including the math and science aspect of coding so that our current and future generations understand what they are building and why. We also need a significant improvement in the humanities. Leaders need to understand how to effectively communicate, lead and listen from a servant-leader perspective. Learning must be as diverse as our human population with the connection component. This means that we need to understand how our individual actions impact others and the world around us so we may act accordingly.

Education will be a personal learning journey as it already is, but we will be more equipped to compensate for learning disabilities through artificial intelligence and delivering learning in a manner best suited for each student. While the basics like reading, writing and arithmetic will remain at the foundation, there will be more free choice and a broader range of topics to develop mindfulness, kindness, and project management at the same time. Empathy and ethics will be at the forefront and critical to our success in building a more United States of America and level the playing field once and for all because we live in an infinite world of limitless possibilities.

Curriculum must include the student. Students will form their own class schedule that is useful and current. We need a realistic education for the real future. We need to stop teaching kids to memorize and teach them to think and make decisions independent of other's opinions. We need to learn to co-create with mother earth and all its inhabitants that are beneficial to the balance of our ecosystem. We need to bring back the trades and home economics; growing our own food, and wood shop. Teach the secrets of the rich like negotiating, asking for discounts and using coupons. We must learn to be flexible, change and adapt to create resilience. This in turn will help us all get through the difficult challenge of taming the student loan dragons and eventually slaying it.

We have a lot of cleaning up to do from plastics clogging our oceans to sustainable drinkable water. If there is among us a future engineer held back by money, then shame on us all. I enjoy the paved roads and buildings, which all involved an engineer. We all have smartphones and social media from engineers too. And who doesn't love food, which is actually very science based and sadly, chemically engineered. When I dial 911 in an emergency, I hope that someone comes to help and there is a doctor to put me back together. The world requires that we have someone we can trust with our lives and our healthcare workers are at the forefront, but they are not taught preventative medicine. Rather, they are taught to treat only symptoms and disease that has been created from a system that extracts your brilliant ideas and turns them into profit machines from themselves while you're left working for a minimum wage that is not a livable wage in this moment.

We also have much healing to do as individuals, communities and society as a whole. We need thought leaders for tomorrow's world of inter-connectedness and inter-dependent countries with as much locally sustained goods and services and less fossil fuel consumed by world travel. There will be a future virtual reality app where you can give a tour of your town to someone else a world away.

The rise of pandemics has forever changed our view of living in a world with bugs that can kill us. We must learn through these new thought leaders that our actions actually can and do affect others and that we're all a little selfish. Others believe there is a finite supply of everything, so they hoard for themselves while others die from starvation. We need to take responsibility for the current world we live in and cease to tolerate the status quo.

Rise up and live as responsible co-creators. We can work, collaborate and reach the world where world leaders, through the United Nations, connects essential sectors such as health, legal, tech, science and engineering to put our brightest minds to work for the benefit of the whole. To do this, we must put aside selfish profits and motives and put an end to the fraud, greed and usury laws favoring capitalism.

Perhaps we shift to a "Capitalism with a Heart" concept. What if we gave our employees a stake in the outcome? What would come from that? How much wealth

What if we had a world full of financially literate people? What if we all fully understood the best way for us to live a good life on a budget and what if that didn't even matter because we all have housing in the future? Imagine a world where it didn't matter what you looked like, but more importantly, the gifts and talents you bring to the world, whatever they may be.

The power that has created the current world, heals the current world. We each have the power within us. We must live a purposeful life, knowing that we have the power to create this new world. What part will you play in that future? How will you speak to others who don't look the same as you do? How will you choose to respond? What education do you need to succeed in this new world?

Imagine if you could meditate and heal your own body. Imagine yourself as part of divine who wants to co-create this future with you, if you would only connect. Imagine a world of mindful, creative people who spread love rather than hate. What education would you need to become supernatural?

Student loan debt is just one barrier to our success and future. We need to tell the truth, take responsibility and educate. We need to develop our own sense of purpose and choose our path without judgment or criticism as long as it contributes. Industries that would lose here, would be big tobacco, anything unsustainable and food that causes disease in the body. We cannot afford to continue on the path we're on or humanity will perish.

We should not have to pay for food, clothing, shelter or drinking water. These are basic needs. We can learn to make our own, but we have no useful skills today. Instead, we are raised to think that we succeed by working for "big corp." and those that have the gold. These same individuals are now the puppet masters, controlling what happens to the money they give. He who has the gold does not have the right to make the rules for all to follow. We the People, the All, must collaborate and unite through our voting powers, to put great thought leaders at the table of decision. What we will see happen is the extinction of human disease when we heal ourselves and then others. Our improved genetics will improve future generations. It's time to unite and heal.

NOTES

Alexandra Hegji, Analyst in Social Policy. *Institutional Eligibility for Participation in Title Iv Student Aid Programs.* Congress (https://crsreports.congress.gov/: February 14, 2019). https://fas.org/sgp/crs/misc/R43159.pdf.

———. *Institutional Eligibility for Participation in Title Iv Student Financial Aid Programs.* (Online: February 14, 2019 2019). https://fas.org/sgp/crs/misc/R43159.pdf.

Bureau, Consumer Financial Protection. "Cfpb Takes Action against National Collegiate Student Loan Trusts, Transworld Systems for Illegal Student Loan Debt Collection Lawsuits." 2017. https://www.consumerfinance.gov/about-us/newsroom/cfpb-takes-action-against-national-collegiate-student-loan-trusts-transworld-systems-illegal-student-loan-debt-collection-lawsuits/.

"California Rosenthal Act." Civil Code, 1977. https://leginfo.legislature.ca.gov/faces/codes_displayText.xhtml?lawCode=CIV&division=3.&title=1.6 C.&part=4.&chapter=&article=1.

Campisi, Jessica. "Sallie Mae Execs Flew over 100 Employees to Hawaii to Celebrate Record $5 Billion in Student Loans: Report." [In English]. *The Hill* (October 18, 2019 2019). https://thehill.com/policy/finance/466492-sallie-mae-execs-flew-over-100-employees-to-hawaii-to-celebrate-record-5#:~:text=In%20August%2C%20Sallie%20Mae%20brought,is%20a%20pretty%20nice%20spot.

209

Code, United States. "Act to Extend the Higher Education Act of 1965." In *Public Law 94-482*, edited by United States Code, 1976. https://uscode.house.gov/statutes/pl/94/482.pdf.

Collinge, Alan Michael. *The Student Loan Scam*. Beacon Press, 2009.

Commission, Federal Trade. "Fair Debt Collection Practices Act." In *X*, edited by FTC.gov, 2010. https://www.ftc.gov/enforcement/rules/rulemaking-regulatory-reform-proceedings/fair-debt-collection-practices-act-text.

———. "Scholarship and Financial Aid Scams." edited by FTC.gov, May, 2012. https://www.consumer.ftc.gov/articles/0082-scholarship-and-financial-aid-scams.

Congress. "National Defense Education Act (Ndea) (P.L. 85-864)." edited by United States Statutes at Large, Vol. 72 p. 1580 - 605, 1958.

Cooper, Preston. "Freopp." In *FREEOPP*, December 2 2020. https://www.kiplinger.com/personal-finance/credit-debt/debt/student-debt/602050/the-best-way-to-pay-off-250000-in-student.

Daley, Terri. "The Conversation." December 2 2020. https://theconversation.com/the-morality-of-canceling-student-debt-150606.

DeMatteo, Megan, "This Is the Average Age When People Finally Pay Off Their Student Loans," CNBC ed., November 25, 2020, 2020, https://www.cnbc.com/select/how-long-it-takes-to-pay-off-student-loans/#:~:text=The%20standard%20repayment%20plan%20for,their%20debt%20within%20a%20decade.

Doom, Professor. "Student Debt 2030: 17 Trillion!", Predictions for future of student loan debt.

World.edu Global Education Network, 2016. https://world.edu/student-debt-2030-17-trillion/.

Education, Office of the Department of. "Federal Student Aid." https://ifap.ed.gov/health-education-assistance-loan-information#:~:text=From%20fiscal%20year%2019 78%20through,chiropractic%2C%20or%20in%20pr ograms%20in.

Education, U.S. Department of. "Diploma Mills and Accreditation; Diploma Mills." 2009. https://www2.ed.gov/students/prep/college/diploma mills/diploma-mills.html.

Efrat, Rafael. "California State University, Northridge." http://www.csun.edu/~re38791/pdfs/Evolution%20o f%20Bankruptcy%20Stigma%20Article.pdf?origin =publication_detail.

Egan, Stephanie Lee and Max. "Student Loans and Student Loan Asset-Backed Securities: A Primer." Primer. *Mondaq* (June 23, 2009 2009). Mondaq. https://www.mondaq.com/unitedstates/banking-finance/81108/student-loans-and-student-loan-asset-backed-securities-a-primer.

Financial Standards. online: Department of Education.

This entry was generated through inserting a Case citation for Homaidan V. Slm Corp. (in Re Homaidan). Case references should appear only in the notes. Remove field codes in the final document and then remove this entry.

Hoppe, Jessica. "Yahoo." In *Yahoo*, December 3 2020. https://www.yahoo.com/lifestyle/student-loans-cancel-debt-keep-153000106.html.

This entry was generated through inserting a Case citation for In Re Birrane. Case references should appear only in the notes. Remove field codes in the final document and then remove this entry.

This entry was generated through inserting a Case citation for In Re Brunner. Case references should appear only in the notes. Remove field codes in the final document and then remove this entry.

This entry was generated through inserting a Case citation for In Re Decena. Case references should appear only in the notes. Remove field codes in the final document and then remove this entry.

Lee, Adam Looney and Vivian. *Parents Are Borrowing More and More to Send Their Kids to College—and Many Are Struggling to Repay.* (Brookings Institution, November 27, 2018). https://www.brookings.edu/research/parents-are-borrowing-more-and-more-to-send-their-kids-to-college-and-many-are-struggling-to-repay/.

Markets, Research and. "Global Online Education Market Worth $319+ Billion by 2025 - North America Anticipated to Provide the Highest Revenue Generating Opportunities." news release, 2020, https://www.globenewswire.com/news-release/2020/04/16/2017102/0/en/Global-Online-Education-Market-Worth-319-Billion-by-2025-North-America-Anticipated-to-Provide-the-Highest-Revenue-Generating-Opportunities.html.

Mayotte, Betsy. "Understand Federal Student Loan Wage Garnishment." *U.S. News & World Report*, July 26, 2017 2017. https://www.usnews.com/education/blogs/student-loan-ranger/articles/2017-07-26/understand-federal-student-loan-wage-garnishment.

Office, U.S. Government Accountability. *Public Loan Forgiveness: Improving the Temporary Expanded Process Could Help Reduce Borrower Confusion.* (Online: U.S. Government Accountability Office,

September 5, 2019 2019). https://www.gao.gov/products/gao-19-595.

Peters, Adele. "The Tech Industry Esacerbated the Housing Crisis. Here's What Google Is Doing to Fix It." *Fast Company*, 2020. https://www.fastcompany.com/90531798/the-tech-industry-exacerbated-the-housing-crisis-heres-what-google-is-doing-to-fix-it.

Requesters, United States Government Accountability Office Report to Congressional. *Public Service Loan Forgiveness; Improving the Temporary Expanded Process Could Help Reduce Borrower Confusion*: United States Government Accountability Office 2019.

Richard Read, Teddy Nykiel, "Feds Point Fingers as 'Debt Relief' Companies Prey on Student Loan Borrowers

" NerdWallet ed., June 14, 2017, 2017, https://www.nerdwallet.com/article/loans/student-loans/debt-relief-companies-prey-student-borrowers.

This entry was generated through inserting a Case citation for Rumer V. American Educational Servs. (in Re Rumer). Case references should appear only in the notes. Remove field codes in the final document and then remove this entry.

Stinson, Sonya. "The Feds Can Garnish Social Security to Pay Your Debts." (December 6, 2017 2017). https://www.bankrate.com/retirement/can-social-security-be-garnished/.

Success, The Institute For College Access &. *Comments on Request for Information Regarding Student Loan Servicing*. online: Consumer Financial Protection Bureau, 2015.

Swaminathon, Aarthi. "Yahoo Finance." In *Yahoo Finance*, December 9 2020.

https://finance.yahoo.com/news/bankruptcy-system-student-loans-reform-bill-210233519.html.

Welsh, Kristy, "Statute of Limitations on Debt; State-by-State Listing," CreditInfocenter ed. *CreditInfocenter*, December 6, 2020, 2020, https://www.creditinfocenter.com/rebuild/statutelimitations.shtml.

Wikipedia. "History of Higher Education in the United States." (2021). https://en.wikipedia.org/wiki/History_of_higher_education_in_the_United_States.

This entry was generated through inserting a Case citation for Williams V. Ecmc. Case references should appear only in the notes. Remove field codes in the final document and then remove this entry.

Bibliography

Bureau, C. F. (2017). *CFPB Takes Action Against National Collegiate Student Loan Trusts, Transworld Systems for Illegal Student Loan Debt Collection Lawsuits*. Retrieved from https://www.consumerfinance.gov/about-us/newsroom/cfpb-takes-action-against-national-collegiate-student-loan-trusts-transworld-systems-illegal-student-loan-debt-collection-lawsuits/

Cooper, P. (2020, December 2). *FREOPP*. Retrieved from FREEOPP: https://www.kiplinger.com/personal-finance/credit-debt/debt/student-debt/602050/the-best-way-to-pay-off-250000-in-student

Daley, T. (2020, December 2). *The Conversation*. Retrieved from https://theconversation.com/the-morality-of-canceling-student-debt-150606

Education, O. o. (n.d.). *Federal Student Aid*. Retrieved from https://ifap.ed.gov/health-education-assistance-loan-information#:~:text=From%20fiscal%20year%201978%20through,chiropractic%2C%20or%20in%20programs%20in

Efrat, R. (n.d.). *California State University, Northridge*. Retrieved from http://www.csun.edu/~re38791/pdfs/Evolution%20o

f%20Bankruptcy%20Stigma%20Article.pdf?origin
=publication_detail

Hoppe, J. (2020, December 3). *Yahoo*. Retrieved from Yahoo: https://www.yahoo.com/lifestyle/student-loans-cancel-debt-keep-153000106.html

https://www.cnbc.com/megan-dematteo/. (2020, December 12). *CNBC*. Retrieved from CNBC: https://www.cnbc.com/select/average-student-loan-debt-by-age/

Swaminathon, A. (2020, December 9). *Yahoo Finance*. Retrieved from Yahoo Finance: https://finance.yahoo.com/news/bankruptcy-system-student-loans-reform-bill-210233519.html

Acknowledgments

I always say, "It takes a village to raise a Christine." I never operate alone. I would like to acknowledge and give credit, where credit is due.

- Cover design: Wyatt Hill, https://hillcreative.design
- Illustrator: Aranea Push, www.araneapush.com
- Book Coach: Dr. Marissa Pei, https://www.drmarissa.life/

I would like to thank my team at Surf City Lawyers for taking care of our clients while I ran off to write this work. I appreciate my work family and look forward to the future of our work together changing lives by eliminating debt.

I would also like to acknowledge Kathryn Atkins, writer. We met while networking many years ago. Since then, she's been a pseudo editor on this and my last book. Mostly, she's been an inspiration for me to write and send my knowledge, experience and thoughts into the universe. She inspires me to change the lives of many versus the few clients I am honored to work with, by writing this book. Without this tribe of supporters, this book would not have come to your hands. In gratitude, for you all.

Resources

- Complaints:
U.S. Department of Education, FSA Ombudsman Group 830 First Street, N.E., Mail Stop 5144, Washington, DC 20202- 5144 Tel: 1-877-557-2575 | Fax: 1-202-275-0549

- Where are my federal student loans: www.nslds.ed.gov

- https://studentaid.gov/manage-loans/repayment/plans/income-driven

- https://www.chea.org/directories

- https://ifap.ed.gov/ifap/fedSchoolCodeList.jsp

- Free Credit Report: www.annualcreditreport.com

- Free Information About Your Student Loan Options: www.studentloanborrowerassistance.org

About the Author

Christine A. Kingston, Esq. is the author of How To Tame The Student Loan Dragon and 5 Steps to Freedom From Debt. Her writings stem from more than a decade in private practice as a consumer bankruptcy lawyer and discharging more than $3 Million in student loans for her clients through bankruptcy and civil litigation defense in California's state courts.

Mrs. Kingston centers her private practice on consumer bankruptcy, litigation in bankruptcy, Fair Debt Collection Practices Act claims, and Fair Credit Reporting Act claims, Attorney Kingston practices in Huntington Beach and surrounding Orange County, Los Angeles, Riverside, and San Bernardino counties. She received her Juris Doctor from Pacific Coast University School of Law (2005), and an undergraduate degree from California State

University, Long Beach (B.A. 1989), where she studied Speech Communication. She is admitted to practice law in California and before the United States District Court, Central District.

Christine is both passionate and compassionate when it comes to helping her clients. She personally works with each client from the beginning of the relationship until a judgment is made. She will assist you with your debt, foreclosure and bankruptcy concerns.

Contact Christine A. Kingston, Esq.:
Surf City Lawyers, APC
5882 Bolsa Avenue, Suite 130
Huntington Beach, California 92649

Tel: 714-533-9210
Email: results@surfcitylawyers.com

www.ingramcontent.com/pod-product-compliance
Lightning Source LLC
Chambersburg PA
CBHW070545010526
44118CB00012B/1230